CONTROL

ACTION STATIONS

10. Supplement and index

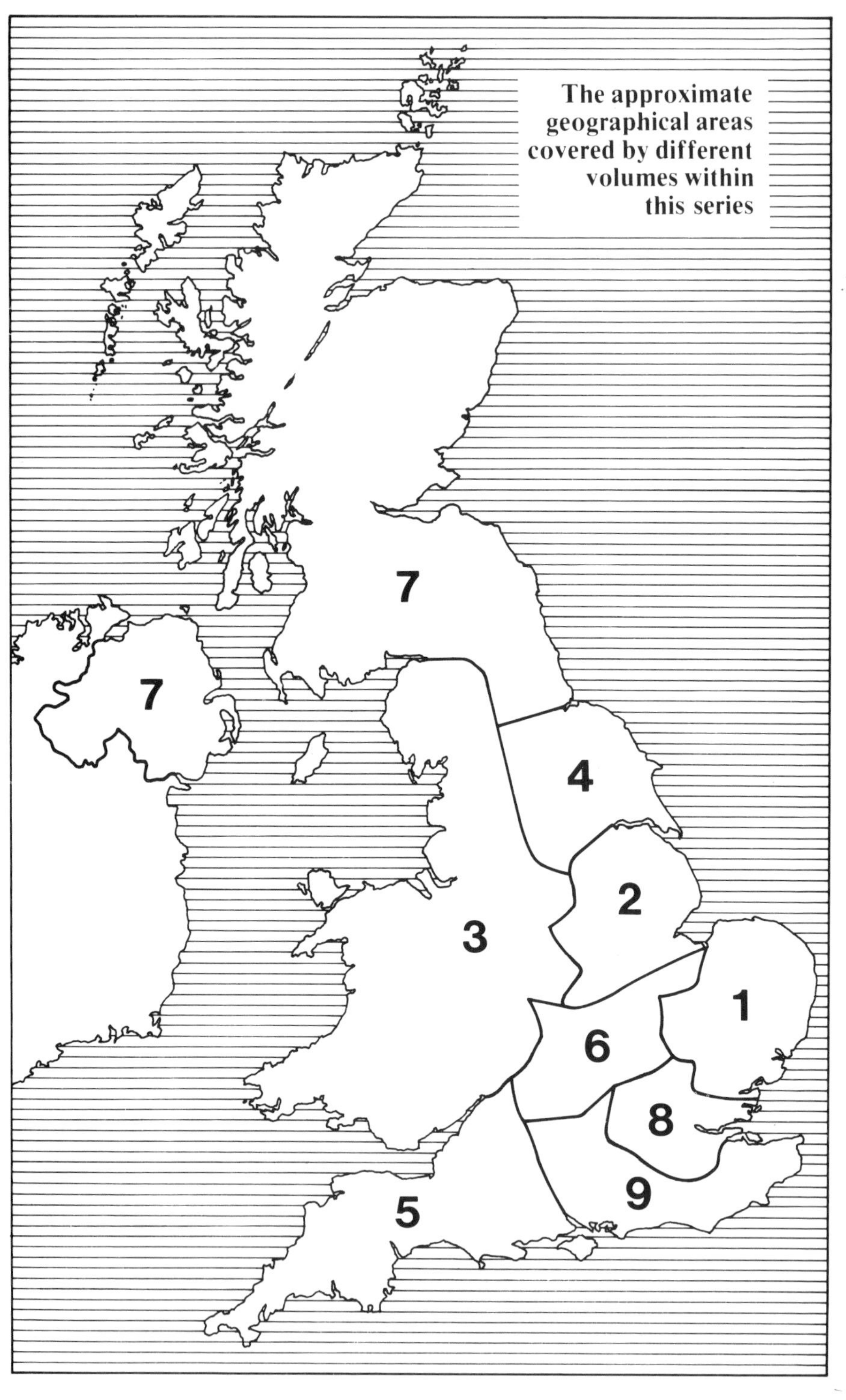
The approximate geographical areas covered by different volumes within this series
7
7
4
2
3
1
6
8
9
5

ACTION STATIONS

10. Supplement and index

COMPILED AND EDITED BY
Bruce Quarrie

Patrick Stephens
Wellingborough, Northamptonshire

First published 1987

British Library Cataloguing in Publication Data

Action stations.—(Action stations; 10)
Supplement and index
1. Air bases—Great Britain—History
I. Quarrie, Bruce II. Series
358.4'17'0941 UG635.G72

ISBN 0-85059-682-3

Patrick Stephens is part of the Thorsons Publishing Group

Printed and bound in Great Britain.

10 9 8 7 6 5 4 3 2

Contents

Introduction

When in April 1979 *Action Stations 1* was published its success was instant. There had been a long gestation period and uncertainty surrounding the extent of interest in a topic about which little had been written. Was there any interest in airfields, many little more than memories? Did they hold fascination only for the aeronautical fraternity?

Answers came fast, verbally and from a shoal of letters recalling people, places, times good and bad at airfields galore. Huge hangars long part of the landscape, decaying huts, runways being smashed to provide hardcore for motorways to link East Anglia via Felixstowe's Container Terminals with the outside world, all were items evoking strong sentiments. Volume 1 appeared synonymously with attempts to preserve remains of items rapidly disappearing, particularly flying control towers, and with the erection of commemorative features. Equally surprising was the increasing interest generally in wartime airfield buildings, those remaining being photographed and nostalgically combed for signs of former glory.

The extent of Volume l's coverage had been subjected to lengthy consideration. East Anglia's uncertain boundaries inevitably led to comments like 'Why was North Weald left out?' and 'Steeple Morden isn't in East Anglia'. Birch clearly held a sacred place in many a heart for letters showered in asking why it had not been included!

Our scheme allowed for approximately 100 airfields in each volume with No 1 carrying introductory features. Eleven volumes were envisaged, each dealing with one area and with a further one carrying a complete index and some up-dating, an aspect that raised problems. Each volume would have an introduction to its area, the series including features on airfield types, buildings, runways, etc. What would not be imposed was an identical style. Instead, a moderately individualistic, easily carried autonomous guide, a complete book for each area, would be devised. One could therefore have in hand brief histories of airfields while visiting any site in the region.

At about the time that Volume 1 was published site plans produced by Air Ministry Works and many aerial photographs of aerodromes became publicly available particularly through the RAF Museum. Photography from high flying Russian nuclear-assisted spy satellites was not only mocking nonsensical 'nuclear free zones', it was also out-dating hitherto secret layouts of British airfields. Many already had no military future, although well into the 1960s over half of East Anglia's aerodromes were still earmarked for development or were standby airfields of some sort. Airfields such as Bradwell Bay, Langham, Lavenham and Shipdham were intended for all-weather fighters, while Sudbury and Rackheath were earmarked for Reserve formations. Although all had long-since been vacated, they retained defence potential. By the 1970s, their value had faded, although within complicated land transactions officialdom makes sure that should the need arise suitable territory could again be requisitioned. While their basic parameters remain unchanged the general toning down in 'smartness' and greatly increased camouflage of many are obvious to any passer by. Disguise is vital for survival in all but a nuclear attack. Protection against terrorism has needed to be much increased in recent years, while irritation caused by protest groups — although small in numbers — means diversion of considerable funds and effort from more useful programmes not necessarily connected with defence. High, protective and extremely expensive fences have had to be erected at some stations for public safety.

When NATO was formed in 1949 the hope was that within 25 years some rapprochement with the Soviet empire could be achieved. Failure to achieve that caused the widespread updating and re-equipment of NATO's air forces and the appearance during the early 1980s of new aircraft types in European skies. Barely a day passes without pairs of ugly, low-flying American Fairchild A-10 anti-tank aircraft cavorting low over the British countryside, using cover skilfully and performing quite amazing manoeuvres in the process. Extensive low flying by fast jets at around 250 ft has also become commonplace over many areas providing sudden noise and unexpected close viewing of Phantoms, Jaguars, Tornados and Hawks as well as foreign F-16s, F-111s and visitors from mainland Europe. Gone are the momentous Vulcans, replaced by Tornados; gone are the purring Devons, just not replaced. Army needs have resulted in the well-being of substantial buildings on one-time permanent RAF airfields. Clearly, the seven years since the first volume of *Action Stations* was published have indeed seen many changes.

One of the most unexpected events was the 1982 Argentinian invasion of the Falklands, and its effects upon many airfield inhabitants were considerable. Within a few days Marham's tankers were practising in-flight refuelling of Waddington's Vulcans whose role as deep penetration bombers had long passed, and soon the Victors were deploying to Ascension to support operations by Nimrods and Vulcans. Harriers from Wittering, Sea Harriers from Yeovilton and helicopters from many sources were soon heading for an unlikely battle scenario. Wyton's Canberras and very secretive Nimrod R 1s also moved to the South Atlantic theatre for operations, all in a manner not seen since the 1956 Suez affair. Brize Norton's VC-10s commenced hectic transport and casevac duties while Marshall Engineering of Cambridge instigated a frantic programme to convert into tankers and receivers a third of the RAF's Hercules fleet. Much indeed has happened since *Action Stations* first appeared, as the following notes concerning many active airfields illustrate.

★ ★ ★

One of the most gratifying aspects of publishing a book is the feedback from readers. If a book is factual then almost inevitably some mistakes are revealed, but far outweighing the knock to one's ego is the value of the additional information freely provided by correspondents. The frustrating thing is that it is impossible to disseminate the 'new' facts, unless a revised edition is issued — or, as in the case of the *Action Stations* series, an 'update' volume is added.

Sometimes a change of emphasis develops as a book series is published, and this is apparent with *Action Stations*. Originally it was thought that the main interest would lie in the World War 2 sites, but it soon became evident that First World War aerodromes held a particular fascination of their own, and the later volumes contain detailed information on landing grounds and marine bases long since closed and largely forgotten. This opportunity has been taken to cover the sites deliberately or inadvertently left out of earlier *Action Stations* volumes as well as to update current airfields — hopefully to good effect.

Individual airfields are dealt with in the same format adopted for the area books, but also included is a detective story — a first class example of what can be discovered by perseverance and by being on the spot (see Sway, Hampshire). We hope this example will prompt others to do the same for their own 'backyards'. There is still much to be documented about wartime airfields, large or small, famous or obscure — *Actions Stations* can only scratch the surface.

As always the staff of the Public Record Office, Air Historical Branch (RAF), Museum of Army Flying, Fleet Air Arm Museum and the RAF Museum have been unfailingly helpful — their assistance is gratefully acknowledged. Official accounts usually make dry reading, however, and are often incomplete. It is then that one relies upon contacts with individuals who were on the spot at the time to put flesh on the bare bones.

Particular mention must be made of the following, but everyone who has taken the trouble to write has added something to the general pool of knowledge and the authors and publishers extend their apologies to anyone whose name has been inadvertently omitted from the following list.

Miss Frances Aldridge, Public Relations Officer, Heathrow, D.Archer, Nigel Bailey-Underwood, E. Barker of British Aerospace, Brough, D. Benfield, R.N.E. Blake, M.J. Burrows, E.F. Cheesman, Captain J.R. Cross, AAC, R.H. Dargue, Sarah Dean, Ian H. Dobinson, Mike Fisher, Neil Fowler, Glynis Fox, Sergeant Terry Goldsmith, Judith Hansom, K.J. Hurst, J.M. Lee, Squadron Leader Ray Leech, G. Mobbs, N. Parker, Pat Otter, M.W. Payne, *RAF News*, Wing Commander Robert J. Sage, OBE, AFC, Terry Senior, Flight Lieutenant J.M. Seymour, Flight Lieutenant Al Stephens, David Utal, K. Wakefield, Jean Walker, K.S. West, Flight Lieutenant Jim Wild, Squadron Leader R.S. Williams and N. Williamson.

Chris Ashworth
Michael Bowyer
Bruce Barrymore Halpenny
Bruce Quarrie
David Smith
August 1987

Glossary

AA Anti-Aircraft
AAC Army Air Corps
AACS Air & Airways Communications Service
AACU Anti-Aircraft Co-operation Unit
A&AEE Aeroplane & Armament Experimental Establishment
AAF Auxiliary Air Force
A&IEU Armament & Instrument Experimental Unit
AAP Aircraft Acceptance Park
AAS Air Armament School
AASF Advanced Air Striking Force
AATT Anti-Aircraft and Target Towing (Flight)
AAU Aircraft Assembly Unit
AC Aero Club; *(AC)* (Army Co-operation)
ACHU Aircrew Holding Unit
ACRC Aircrew Reselection Centre
ADDL Aerodrome Dummy Deck Landing
ADEE Air Defence Experimental Establishment
ADF Air Defence Squadron
ADG Air Depot Group
ADGB Air Defence of Great Britain
ADU Air Disarmament Unit
AEF Air Experience Flight
AERE Atomic Energy Research Establishment
AES Air Electrical School
AEW Airborne Early Warning
AFB Air Force Base (USAF)
AFDS Air Fighting Development Squadron
AFDU Air Fighting Development Unit
AFEE Airborne Forces Experimental Establishment
AFS Advanced Flying School
AFSC Air Force Service Command (USAAF)
AFTCC Air Force Troop Carrier Command
AFTS Advanced Flying Training School
AGS Air Gunnery School
AHU Aircraft Holding Unit
AI Airborne Interception (radar)
AMWD Air Ministry Works Department
ANS Air Navigation School
Anti-diver Patrol to shoot down V-1 flying bombs
Anti-rhubarb Patrol to intercept low-level intruders
Anvil Amphibious invasion of southern France in 1944
AOC Air Officer Commanding
AONS Air Observer Navigation School
AOP Air Observation Post
AOS Air Observer School
APC Armament Practice Camp
Aphrodite Use of aged aircraft as radio-controlled bombers
APS Armament Practice Station
ARDU Aircraft Receipt & Despatch Unit
A/S Anti-Submarine
ASC Air Support Command
ASH Narrow-beam radar used for low-level operations
ASI Air Speed Indicated *or* Indicator
ASL Above Sea Level
ASR Air-Sea Rescue
AST Air Service Training
ASU Aircraft Storage Unit
ASWDU Air-Sea Warfare Development Unit
ASV Air-to-Surface Vessel (radar)
ATA Air Transport Auxiliary
ATC Air Training Corps *or* Air Traffic Control
ATG Air Transport Group
ATDU Air Torpedo Development Unit
ATrDU Air Transport Development Unit
ATS Armament Training Station *or* Air Training Squadron
ATTDU Airborne Tactical Transport Development Unit
AWDS All-Weather Development Squadron
AWFCS All-Weather Fighter Combat Squadron
AWRE Atomic Weapons Research Establishment

BA British Airways
BABS Blind Approach Beam System
Baedecker raid German reprisal attack delivered on historical city
BAFO British Air Forces of Occupation
BAT Flight Blind *or* Beam Approach Training Flight
BCBS Bomber Command Bombing School
BCIS Bomber Command Instructors' School
BCDU Bomber Command Development Unit
BDTF Bomber Defence Training Flight
BDU Bomber Development Unit
BEA British European Airways
BEF British Expeditionary Force
Bellicose Code name for first shuttle raid in June 1943
BFTS Basic Flying Training School
BG Bomb Group (USAAF)
B&G Bombing & Gunnery (Flight)
BLEU Blind Landing Experimental Unit
BMEWS Ballistic Missile Early Warning System
BOAC British Overseas Airways Corporation
BS Bomb Squadron (USAAF)
BSDU Bomber Support Development Unit
BTU Bombing Trials Unit
Bullseye Night training exercise for bomber and defence personnel

BW Bomb Wing (USAAF)
CAACU Civilian Anti-Aircraft Co-operation Unit
Cab Rank Fighter bombers on immediate call for close support of the Army
CACU Coastal Artillery Co-operation Unit
CAG Civil Air Guard *or* Carrier Air Group
Calvert Bar landing light system A system of bars and intervening lights leading to runway threshold
CAM (ship) Catapult Aircraft Merchant (ship)
CANS Civil Air Navigation School
Carpet Supply-dropping operation to resistance forces
CATCS Central Air Traffic Control School
CCDU Coastal Command Development Unit
CCFIS Coastal Command Flying Instructors' School
CCGP Coastal Command Group Pool
CCRC Combat Crew Replacement Center (USAAF)
CFE Central Fighter Establishment
CFS Central Flying School
CGS Central Gunnery School
CH Chain Home (radar station)
Channel Stop Attempt to close the English Channel to enemy shipping
Chastise Code name for the Dams raid by 617 Squadron in May 1943
Circus Fighter-escorted operation to entice enemy response
CLE Central Landing Establishment
C&M Care & Maintenance
CNCS Central Navigation & Control School
CND Campaign for Nuclear Disarmament
CONUS Continental United States — USAF supply organisation
Cork Coastal Command A/S operation, 1944
COT Flight Czech Operational Training Flight
CPF Coastal Patrol Flight
Crossbow Code name for the campaign against V-weapons
CSE Central Signals Establishment
CTW Combat Training Wing
CU Conversion Unit
Darkie system Method of homing at night on radio signals
Day Ranger Operation to engage air and ground targets within a wide but specified area, by day
DFCS Day Fighter Combat School
Dicer Low-level photo reconnaissance sortie
Distil Fighter operation to shoot down enemy aircraft minesweeping, usually off Denmark
Diver A V-1 flying bomb
DME Distance Measuring Equipment
Dodge Operation to ferry troops home from Italy
Drem lighting System of outer markers and approach lights installed at many airfields in the early years of the war
DZ Dropping Zone
E/A Enemy Aircraft
EATS Empire Air Training Scheme
EBTS Elementary and Basic Training School (Coastal Command)
ECFS Empire Central Flying School
ECM Electronic Counter-Measures
EFTS Elementary Flying Training School
EGS Elementary Glider School
ELG Emergency Landing Ground
ENSA Entertainments National Service Association
E&RFTS Elementary & Reserve Flying Training School
Eric Day training exercise for bomber and fighter crews
Erpr Erprobungsgruppe (German experimental group)
ETO European Theatre of Operations
E&WS Electrical & Wireless School
Exodus Ferrying troops and displaced person to and from Europe
FAA Fleet Air Arm
FAW Fleet Air Wing (US Navy)
FBFU Flying Boat Fitting Unit
FBSU Flying Boat Servicing Unit
FBTS Flying Boat Training Squadron
FBG Fighter Bomber Group (USAAF)
FG Fighter Group (USAAF)
FIDO Fog Investigation and Dispersal Operation
Fighter Night Fighter patrol over area where anti-aircraft gunners were ordered not to fire, sometimes restricted to certain altitudes
Firebash Sorties by Mosquitoes of 100 Group with the aircraft delivering incendiary or napalm loads on German airfields
FIS Flying Instructors' School
FIU Fighter Interception Unit
Flak *Fl*ieger*a*bwehr*k*annon (German AA fire)
FLS Fighter Leaders' School
FPP Ferry Pilots Pool
FPU Flying Practice Unit
FRU Fleet Requirements Unit (FAA) *or* Forward Repair Unit (RAF)
FS Ferry *or* Fighter Squadron (USAAF)
FSP Forward Staging Post
FTS Flying Training School
FTU Ferry Training Unit
FU Ferry Unit
Fuller Counter-measures against the escape of the *Scharnhorst* and *Gneisenau* from Brest
Gardening Code name for sea minelaying by aircraft
GCA Ground-Controlled Approach
GCI Ground-Controlled Interception
Gee Medium-range radio aid to navigation equipment employing ground transmitters and airborne receivers
GP (bomb) General Purpose high explosive bomb
GRU General Reconnaissance Unit *or* Gunnery Research Unit
GS Glider School (ATC)
GSU Group Support *or* Standardisation Unit
GTS Glider Training School
Haddock Code name for a force of Wellingtons sent to the south of France in 1940 to bomb Italy
HCU Heavy Conversion Unit
HE High Explosive
HFF Heavy Freight Flight
HGCU Heavy Glider Conversion Unit
HGMU Heavy Glider Maintenance Unit
Highball Bouncing bomb designed to fit the Mosquito
HTCU Heavy Transport Conversion Unit
H2S Airborne radar navigational and target location aid
ICBM Inter-Continental Ballistic Missile
IE Initial Equipment
IFF Identification Friend or Foe
IFTU Intensive Flying Trials Unit
IHTU Inter-Service Hovercraft Trials Unit
Intruder Offensive night operation to fixed point or specified target
IR Immediate Reserve
IRBM Intermediate Range Ballistic Missile
ITS Initial *or* Intermediate Training School
ITW Initial Training Wing
JG Jagdgeschwader (German fighter wing)
Jim Crow Reconnaissance patrols by armed fighters
JOAC Junior Officers' Air Course
Jubilee Combined operations at Dieppe, 1942

KB Kite Balloon
KG Kampfgeschwader (German bomber wing)
LAA Light Anti-Aircraft
Lagoon Shipping reconnaissance operation off the Dutch coast
Leigh light Searchlight for A/S operations
LFS Lancaster Finishing School
LG Landing Ground *or* Lehrgeschwader (German operational training unit)
Lindholme gear Equipment dropped from ASR aircraft to crews ditched in the sea, developed at RAF Lindholme
Link trainer Early flight simulator for training
LNSF Light Night Striking Force
Lorenz system Blind beam approach system
LRDF Long Range Development Flight
LTU Loran Training Unit
MAEE Marine Aircraft Experimental Establishment
Mahmoud Night fighter sortie to specific point over enemy territory to engage his night fighters in that area
Mallard Final airborne phase of *Overlord*
Mandrel Airborne radar jamming device used by 100 Group
Manna Delivery of food and supplies to Holland in 1945
MAP Ministry of Aircraft Production
Market Airborne operation at Arnhem, 1944
MATS Military Air Transport Service
MCA Ministry of Civil Aviation
MCU Mosquito Conversion Unit *or* Marine Craft Unit
MDAP Mutual Defence Aid Programme
METS Multi-Engined Training Squadron
Millennium First 1,000-bomber raid on Cologne in May 1942
MoA Ministry of Aviation
MoD Ministry of Defence
MOTU Maritime Operational Training Unit
MR squadron Maritime *or* Medium Reconnaissance squadron
MRU Mountain Rescue Unit
MSFU Merchant Ship Fighter Unit
MT Mechanical *or* Motor Transport
MTCA Ministry of Transport and Civil Aviation
MU Maintenance Unit
Musketeer Code name for the Suez operation in 1956
NAAFI Navy, Army, Air Force Institute
NAFDU Naval Air Fighting Development Unit
NATO North Atlantic Treaty Organisation
Neptune Naval side of *Overlord*
Nickelling Leaflet dropping
Night Ranger Operation to engage, air and ground targets within a wide but specified area, at night
Noball A V-1 or V-2 site
OADF Overseas Air Delivery Flight
OADU Overseas Aircraft Despatch Unit
(O)AFU Observers Advanced Flying Unit
OAPU Overseas Aircraft Preparation Unit
Oboe Ground-controlled radar system of blind bombing in which one station indicated track to be followed and another the bomb release point
OCTU Officer Cadet Training Unit
OCU Operational Conversion Unit
(O)FIS (Operational) Flying Instructors' School
OFU Overseas Ferry Unit
ORB Operations Record Book
ORTU Operational Refresher Training Unit
OTU Operational Training Unit
Overlord Code-name for D-Day
PAC Parachute and Cable (installation)
(P)AFU (Pilots) Advanced Flying Unit
PAMPA Long-range weather reporting sortie
PDC Personnel Despatch Centre
PFF Pathfinder Force
PFFNTU Pathfinder Force Navigational Training Unit
PFS Primary Flying Squadron
PIR Parachute Infantry Regiment (US)
POL Petrol, Oil and Lubricants
PoW Prisoner of War
Prata Weather reconnaissance flight
PRU Photographic Reconnaissance Unit
PSP Pierced Steel Planking (runway)
PTS Parachute Training School
Pundit Lights or letters displayed giving the airfield identity code
PX Post Exchange (US canteen/shop)
Q-site A site flashing lights to represent a mock airfield to attract enemy attention at night
RAAF Royal Australian Air Force
RAE Royal Aircraft Establishment
RAeC Royal Aero Club
RAFA Royal Air Force Association
RAFC Royal Artillery Flying Club
RAFGSA RAF Gliding and Soaring Association
RAFVR RAF Volunteer Reserve
Ramrod Bomber raid escorted by fighters aimed at destruction of a particular target in daylight
Ranger Usually a deep penetration flight to a specified area, to engage targets of opportunity
RAS Reserve Aeroplane Squadron
RAT Flight Radio Aids Training Flight
RAuxAF Royal Auxiliary Air Force
RAW Royal Airship Works
RC Recruit Centre
RCAF Royal Canadian Air Force
RCM Radio Counter-Measures (squadron or flight)
RDF Radio Direction Finding
Reflex American SAC bomber detachments on ground alert at overseas bases
RF Reserve Flight
RFC Royal Flying Corps
RFS Reserve Flying School
Rhombus Weather reporting flight
Rhubarb Low-level strike operation mounted in cloudy conditions against enemy targets in occupied countries
RLG Relief Landing Ground
RNAS Royal Naval Air Station *or* Service
RNZAF Royal New Zealand Air Force
RNEFTS Royal Navy Elementary Flying Training School
RNVR Royal Naval Volunteer Reserve
Roadstead Fighter operation against shipping
Robinson Lancaster raid on Le Creusot in October 1942
ROC Royal Observer Corps
Rodeo Fighter sweep
Rover Coastal Command armed patrol to search for enemy shipping
RRE Royal Radar Establishment
RS Reserve Squadron
RTC Recruit Training Centre
Rutter Abandoned attack on German heavy guns at Dieppe in July 1942
SAC Strategic Air Command
SAH School of Aircraft Handling
SAM Surface-to-Air Missile
SAN School of Air Navigation
Saracen Scheme under which all fighter OTUs would be turned into operational squadrons in the event of invasion
SAS Special Air Service
Sashlite bulb Photo-flash bulb used for training and experimental purposes

SBA Standard Beam Approach
SBAC Society of British Aircraft Constructors
SBC Small Bomb Container
Scatter scheme Temporary withdrawal of operational squadrons to rearward bases on outbreak of war
SDF Special Duty Flight
Serrate Sortie to locate and destroy enemy night fighters and combined with night bomber raids; made use of airborne radar
SF Servicing Flight
SFTS Service Flying Training School
SHAEF Supreme Headquarters Allied Expeditionary Force
SHQ Supreme *or* Station Headquarters
SLG Satellite Landing Ground
SMT Square Mesh Track (runway)
SOC Struck Off Charge
SOE Special Operations Executive
SofAC School of Army Co-operation
SofAG School of Aerial Gunnery
SofFC School of Flying Control
SofGR School of General Reconnaissance
SofN&BD School of Navigation and Bomb Dropping
SofNC School of Naval Co-operation
SofTT School of Technical Training
Sommerfeld tracking Wire mesh runway material
Spartan Exercise to establish methods of making an entire airfield formation mobile
SPTU Staff Pilot Training Unit
SRW Strategic Reconnaissance Wing
SSS Sub-Storage Site
Starfish Dummy fire to attract attention away from an important target
Starkey Large-scale 'spoof' invasion of the Pas de Calais in September 1943, made to assess German reactions and bring their fighters to battle
StG Stukageschwader (Ju 87 wing)
Stopper Coastal Command patrol outside Brest harbour
STT School of Technical Training
SU Signals Unit *or* Servicing Unit
Sunray Overseas training flight for bomber crews
TAC Tactical Air Command (USAAF)
TAF Tactical Air Force
TAMU Transport Aircraft Maintenance *or* Modification Unit
TAW Tactical Airlift Wing (USAF)
TBR Torpedo Bomber Reconnaissance
TCDU Transport Command Development Unit
TCU Transport Conversion Unit
TCW Troop Carrier Wing (also Group and Squadron)
TDS Training Depot Station
TDU Torpedo Development Unit
TDY Temporary Duty Overseas (USAF)
TEU Tactical Exercise Unit
TF Training Flight
TFU Telecommunications Flying Unit
TFW Tactical Fighter Wing
Thum Weather reporting flight
TI Target Indicator
Tiger Force British bombing force for operations against Japan
Torch Invasion of French North Africa in November 1942
Totalize Canadian offensive at Falaise in August 1944
TRE Telecommunications Research Establishment
TRG Tactical Reconnaissance Group
TRS Tactical Reconnaissance Squadron *or* Torpedo Refresher Squadron
TS Training Squadron
TSCU Transport Support Conversion Unit
TTC Technical Training Command
TTF Target Towing Flight
TTTE Tri-National Tornado Training Establishment
TTU Torpedo Training Unit
Turbinlite Airborne searchlight for night fighter operations
TWU Tactical Weapons Unit
UAS University Air Squadron
UP A projector for firing Z rockets
USAAC US Army Air Corps
USAAF US Army Air Force (from June 20 1941)
USAF US Air Force (postwar)
USAFE US Air Force Europe
USAS United States Air Service
Varsity Airborne operation to facilitate the crossing of the Rhine in March 1945
VOR VHF Omni-directional Receiver
V/STOL Vertical/Short Take Off and Landing
WAAF/WRAF Womens Auxiliary/Royal Air Force
WAEC War Emergency Agricultural Committee
WD War Department
Window Metallised paper strips dropped by bombers to disrupt enemy radar systems
WRNS Womens Royal Naval Service
WS Wireless School
X-raid Approaching unidentified aircraft
Y-Service British organisation monitoring German radio transmissions to and from aircraft
ZG Zerstörer (German destroyer, ship or — usually — twin-engined aircraft)

The airfields

Roman numerals following a heading denote the *Action Stations* volume in which the original entry appeared. Airfields without such a number are 'new' to this volume.

Abbots Bromley, Staffordshire (III)

First used between mid-1940 and December 1941 by 5 EFTS, Meir.

Abbotsinch, Strathclyde (VII)

A Callender-Hamilton hangar close to the terminal is used for airport vehicles. Loganair use the adjacent 'C' type.

Aberporth, Dyfed (III)

Used from September 1939 by 'X' Flight 1 AACU but was certainly open from at least a year before.

Acklington, Northumberland (VII)

Allocated to the 8th Air Force for tactical fighter use on July 12 1943 but never occupied by them. Decoy Q-site was at Longhoughton.

Alconbury, Cambridgeshire (I)

TL213768.

Alconbury of 1945 included the customary three concrete and asphalt runways, 24/06 1,925 yd long and two others of 1,500 yd. It had 50 loop-type hardstandings and two 'T2' hangars. In the first major evaluation of airfields for possible future development, undertaken during January 1947, the choice included among the less likely ones Hardwick, King's Cliffe, Sibson, Shepherd's Grove and Wethersfield. Very complex air

Acklington in August 1968. Left to right—two 'F' Type hangars, a 'D' Type and a 'T2' (J. Huggon).

Master and Hurricanes at Annan, circa 1943 (via Chris Thomas).

defence expansion schemes followed, each the subject of constant revision, and during 1953 the Americans agreed to develop Alconbury, Congress approving funding for a new, long runway to replace the existing 065/245. Two years were allocated for the up-dating during which plans were made for Alconbury, in the event of war, to house the F-84 Thunderjets from Manston which would be replaced there by an RAF all-weather fighter squadron in addition to the station's use as an advanced fighter base for Allied forces. The Americans intended Alconbury otherwise to be an Air Depot with an asphalt Runway 12/30 of 9,009 ft and eventually an increased assortment of hangars.

Alconbury remains firmly in USAF hands, although RF-4Cs of the 1st Tactical Reconnaissance Squadron, 10th TRW, left June 1987. Periodically Alconbury hosts transit aircraft, and squadrons still come to be trained in aerial combat by the 527th TFTAS, activated here on April 1 1976 and assigned to the 10th TRW. It received the first of 20 F-5E Tigers on 21 May 1976 which became operational on July 1 1977 and remain a common sight. The main change has been the activation on October 1 1982, and slow expansion, of the 95th Reconnaissance Squadron, 17th Reconnaissance Wing, steadily increasing towards a strength of 17 of the strange-looking, all-black Lockheed TR-1s. Quiet jets, the first of which arrived on February 12 1983, they look more like giant sailplanes than highly sophisticated, ultra high-flying and much sensorised battle surveillance reconnaissance aircraft.

Aldergrove, Antrim (VII)

The date of the air raid on the Belfast area in which an He 111 was shot down was April 7/8 1941.

Andrewsfield (Great Saling), Essex (I)

TL687247. 4 miles WNW of Braintree

Great Saling ended the war as a Fighter Command Forward Airfield in the North Weald Sector. It had the customary 2,000 × 50 yd runway (09/27) and two 1,400-yd runways all of concrete and topped with tarmac and wood chips. There were two 'T2' hangars and 50 loop hardstandings.

Andrewsfield is now an active private airfield operated by Andrewsfield Flying Club Ltd, and attracts an assortment of present day light civil aircraft which use runway 09/27 which is now a grass strip 2,362 ft long and 79 ft wide.

Annan, Dumfries and Galloway (VII)

Another fighter OTU station in this area was planned at Robgill with satellite at Caerlaverock but was never built.

Anthorn, Cumbria (III)

The first aircraft to arrive for the ARDU was Barracuda *DR212* from Easthaven on September 25 1944. Construction of the airfield proved difficult because of extensive areas of peat. An apochryphal story has it that a steam-roller became bogged down and as it proved virtually impossible to remove it, it was allowed to settle and now reposes under the intersection of the runways. Hence the expression 'roller landings'!

The site was prepared originally as a grass landing ground for the RAF but relinquished to the Admiralty in December 1942.

Arbroath, Tayside (VII)

During an air raid by two He 111s and one Do 215 on October 25 1940 a squadron office was demolished and two other buildings had their roofs blown off. The station defence consisted mainly of Army-manned Lewis guns who unfortunately thought the enemy aircraft were friendly and about to land so did not fire a shot until it was too late. On March 8 1941 King George VI visited the station and planted a tree just inside the gate to mark his visit. Three air-firing ranges were operated: in Lunan Bay, off Stonehaven, and off Arbroath. In 1942 visiting squadrons were located at various sites around the aerodrome, the aircraft being housed in Dutch barns. This was done to minimise damage from future attacks but the Luftwaffe made no further appearances.

Ashbourne, Derbyshire (III)
When 42 OTU disbanded some of its surplus Albemarles were pushed into an abandoned quarry which was then filled in.

Aston Down (Minchinhampton), Gloucestershire
See Minchinhampton.

Atcham, Salop (III)
The accident rate for the 495th FTG was so high that questions were asked even as far away as Washington DC. Between January 1 and October 31 1944, 157 aircraft were involved in 137 accidents, resulting in 37 fatalities. Staff at Atcham considered that much was due to the generally poor standard of training pilots had received in the USA prior to going overseas. Other factors were the high ground in the vicinity, war-weary aircraft and frequent bad weather.

Ayr (Heathfield) Strathclyde (VII)
Allocated to the 8th Air Force as a tactical fighter base on July 12 1943 but never occupied. Audaxes towing Hotspur gliders were based here for a short period circa 1943, reason unknown. A single Bellman hangar remains and is now used as a fertiliser store.

Ayr (racecourse), Strathclyde (VII)
No 1 School of Aerial Fighting formed here on September 17 1917 and disbanded on May 10 1918. North Western Area Flying Instructors' School formed here on July 1 1918.

Balado Bridge, Tayside (VII)
The tower still stands in the middle of a cultivated field and is thus inaccessible for much of the year. Permission must be sought from the farmer to view.

Ballyhalbert, Down (VII)
There were eventually 12 Blister hangars here. The correct spelling of the decoy site is Kearney. No 504 Squadron arrived on *August* 26 1941. Allocated tentatively for USAAF Air Support Command February 28 1942, then on September 26 1942 as USAAF fighter base but cancelled April 1943. Allocated 8th Air Force for tactical fighters as lodger units July 12 1943 but never occupied. No 24 Naval Fighter Wing consisted of 887 and 894 Squadrons, No 3 Naval Fighter Wing of 808 and 885 Squadrons.

Ballykelly, Londonderry (VII)
Planned pre-war as an Aircraft Storage Unit but rejected because of drainage difficulties. On further review it was considered that the problem could be overcome so a contract was let to Messrs B. Sunley & Co in December 1940, by which time a more active role was envisaged.

Banff, Grampian (VII)
No 248 Squadron did not disband here but moved to Chivenor July 19 1945. The Strike Wing's anti-shipping 'scoreboard' is still to be seen in the ops room along with other faded inscriptions.

Bangor, Gwynedd (III)
In existence from June 1918 to early

Aircrew with Liberator BZ724 *of 59 Squadron at Ballykelly in March 1944. This aircraft crashed near Helmsdale, Sutherland, on January 18 1944 whilst diverting to Tain in bad weather. Some wreckage remains at the site* (via J.D. Oughton).

spring of 1919 for DH 6s of 244 Squadron. Anti-U-boat patrols were flown from Bangor around Anglesey and the North Wales coast.

Barkston Heath, Lincolnshire (II)

In early 1983 it was decided to transfer Bloodhound anti-aircraft missiles from Germany to Barkston Heath, just 20 miles from Lincoln. For security reasons the number of missiles at the base has not been made known. Redeployment of missiles from Germany started in October 1981 to a number of East Anglian sites. The Bloodhounds have been replaced in Germany by Rapier missiles.

Barkston Heath also has a wartime link for it houses the Consolidated PBY Catalina amphibian which, during 1985, appeared at airshows up and down the country. It also starred in a television series filmed in Norway. The 'Cat', former US Navy aircraft *CF-MIR*, is the only operational Catalina in Europe.

After 40 years there are few Catalinas still in operation and it was very fortunate that Flight Lieutenants John Watts and Paul Warren-Wilson and aerial photographer Arther Gibson obtained *CF-MIR* from a Canadian survey company in February 1985. It was flown to Barkston Heath from South Africa.

The Catalina is fittingly painted in the wartime markings of Flying Officer John Alexander Cruickshank's 210 Squadron aircraft in which he earned a Victoria Cross (see also Sullom Voe). On July 17 1944 Cruickshank was the captain and pilot of a Catalina flying boat which was on sea patrol in northern waters. He attacked a U-boat lying on the surface and his Catalina came under intense fire and was repeatedly hit. The navigator and bomb-aimer were killed and the co-pilot and two side gunners injured. Cruickshank was hit in 72 places, receiving two serious wounds in the lungs and ten serious wounds in the lower limbs. Regardless of his injuries he pressed home his attack and released the depth charges himself. The U-boat was sunk under the determined attack. In intense pain, Cruickshank brought the Catalina back to safety. Despite the number and severity of his wounds he survived.

The airfield is still in a good state of repair and its role remains as a RLG for Royal Air Force Cranwell.

Barrow (Walney Island), Cumbria (III)

Originally planned as a forward fighter aerodrome for 9 Group. No 188 Gliding School was present here from early 1947 until at least September 1949.

Barton, Greater Manchester (III)

Correct opening date was January 1 1930. No 2 RFS was present from October 1948 until March 1953. No 185 GS formed here

The Catalina flying boat from Barkston Heath.

by March 1944, and suspended operations in December 1947.

Bassingbourn, Cambridgeshire (I)

Bassingbourn has ceased to be an airfield, but the links with past days are recalled in a museum in the pre-war control tower which was much modified for wartime use, probably in 1942. It contains hosts of photographs and exhibits which have been gathered by the East Anglian Aviation Society. They portray Bassingbourn's history and also that of the Steeple Morden satellite. The ground floor is devoted to the RAF and, as well as exhibits of local interest, also houses some unusual gifts, among them the wind tunnel model of the Warwick bomber featuring remotely controlled guns in its engine nacelles. Upstairs is devoted to the USAAF and carries an excellent collection of 'local' photographs, with sections also portraying Steeple Morden and Duxford. Among other items is a cotton flag inscribed in Russian and brought home after the 91st Bomb Group indulged in shuttle bombing.

Bassingbourn, though, is the Army's Queen's Division Depot and therefore access is understandably restricted. Before contemplating a call may I suggest that you contact Vince Hemmings, the Curator, on Letchworth 673340?

Beaulieu, Hants (V)

Brief mention of the First World War aerodrome at Beaulieu has already been made, but space precluded any detail. The New Forest Flying School ceased operations at its Beaulieu aerodrome *(SU369010)* in January 1912 when the aeroplanes were put up for sale. The sheds remained, however, and were offered to the RFC with the aerodrome in November 1913. The site was inspected by officers from Farnborough, but subsequently rejected because of the poor emergency landing facilities in the area. Within a few months the international situation had changed, however, and so had attitudes, the War Office taking out a lease on one of the sheds. It was little used and Beaulieu remained abandoned until the autumn of 1915 when a desperate need for more flying schools resulted in permission being sought for the re-opening of the old landing ground.

The locals raised no objection, indeed Lord Montagu, the most influential amongst them, was positively in favour.

RE 8 A4552 *at Beaulieu, probably a machine belonging to No 16 Reserve School. In the background can be seen some of the Bessoneaux canvas-covered hangars so common on World War 1 aerodromes* (RAF Museum, PO14502).

So it was not long before a T-shaped area of ground was marked out, just south of Hatchet Pond and between the Beaulieu-Lymington road and the Beaulieu Rails. The first machine arrived on December 17 1915, the same day as No 16 Reserve Squadron was formed at Beaulieu.

By the end of January 1916 wooden huts and sheds proliferated and the landing ground was soon found to be too small. It underwent several changes in size and shape before finishing up with almost the same dimensions as that opened in 1910 for the New Forest Flying School! It was much improved, however, the scrub and heather being cleared and the ground levelled by the back-breaking work of Chinese labourers.

During June the nucleus of No 23 RS was formed from 16 RS personnel before going to Aboukir, Egypt, in August with BE 2Cs. This aircraft was also widely used by the parent 16 RS at this time alongside the inevitable Avro 504s. In January 1917 No 84 Squadron, theoretically an operational scout unit, formed at Beaulieu and used BE 2 variants for training before moving to Lilbourne near Rugby for final work-up prior to re-equipping with SE 5As and crossing to France in September. The nucleus of No 87 RS, a unit working up in readiness for transfer to Canada, arrived from Gosport during February but was soon aboard ship, leaving a small number of Curtiss JN-4 Jenny trainers behind for 16 RS to use alongside their BE 2Cs, DH 6s and RE 8s. All these machines suffered badly from the attentions of the pupils. Accidents were commonplace, the combination of frequent gusty winds and a poorly drained surface resulting in many spectacular 'arrivals'. Usually the damage was confined to the removal of the undercarriage or a battering when the machine overturned, but there were injuries and some fatalities, inevitable in any high-pressure training environment.

At the end of May the Reserve Squadrons were all renamed Training Squadrons, and to confuse the issue the 'operational' No 79 Squadron arrived from Gosport on August 4 to act as a training unit until December, when work-up commenced on the new Sopwith Dolphin before going to France in February 1918. This almost constant succession of new units continued with No 103 Squadron, which had formed at Beaulieu on September 1 1917 as a day bomber outfit, but only stayed a week before moving to Old Sarum, and then after nearly two years on the aerodrome No 16 RS swopped places with No 59 TS, going to Yatesbury on November 30. The purpose of this exchange remains unclear for both units had similar tasks and aircraft.

No 59 TS did not stay long, however, going to Lilbourne early in 1918 having been replaced by Nos 1 and 70 TS which operated Pups and Camels at Beaulieu as part of the 17th Wing, Southern Training Brigade, alongside No 117 Sqn, a day bomber squadron formed on New Year's Day 1918 and equipped with DH 4 and RE 8 aircraft. They were joined by the Avro 504s and Pups of 73 TS in February when the station was in the throes of a massive building programme involving the construction of four 170 ft × 100 ft GS hangars on the western side and additions to the original technical site near East Boldre. A new domestic site to the south-west of the landing ground provided much needed extra accommodation, a large wire-fenced compound housing a women's hostel on the opposite side of the Lymington road to the officer's and men's huts. The Women's Army Auxiliary Corps were employed as drivers, waitresses, cooks, typists, fabric workers and even as airframe riggers. They became part of the Women's Royal Air Force in April 1918.

Considerable re-organisation followed the creation of the RAF, resulting in much shuffling of units to allow pairs of Training Squadrons to amalgamate to form Training Depot Stations. No 1 and part of No 73 TS became No 29 TDS at Beaulieu on July 27, while No 70 and the rest of 73 TS went to South Carlton to join No 28 TDS. The establishment of the new unit at Beaulieu was 36 Avro 504K trainers and 36 Dolphin scouts but Camels remained on strength until sufficient Dolphins became available.

The building programme was almost complete at the end of the war and the aerodrome continued in use into 1919 while No 29 TDS gradually faded away. Contractors' plant and equipment was removed in July and two months later the buildings were put up for sale by the Aerodrome Disposal Board. For a time Lymington RDC showed interest in the domestic accommodation as temporary housing but eventually everything, including the hangars, went 'under the hammer' during 1920. Dismantling quickly followed, leaving acres of concrete foundations which were not completely removed until 1924. Just one building survives on its original site, the YMCA hut which is now East Boldre village hall.

Beaumaris, Anglesey (III)

RAF Coronado flying boats were also handled here. Beside the slipway a slot has been cut in the wall to allow a Catalina float to pass through. The 'T2' and 'B1' hangars are still in use for naval contract work so access to the site is actively discouraged. Other aircraft types seen here during the war were the floatplane Spitfire, Sea Foxes and the Shetland flying boat.

Beccles (Ellough), Suffolk (I)

Few things in life are better than contemplation of what might have been. The long-time retention of the runway at Beccles is explained by the fact that into the mid-1950s it was listed as a potential fighter station, like Great Massingham and Nuthampstead. Similar lengthy lives of Chelveston, Lavenham, Gransden and Polebrook which, with Tuddenham in the 1960s was a Thor site, came about because each of these was retained for possible development as a bomber base. Hardly surprising when one discovers that early production plans for the Avro Vulcan called for 1,000 examples—and more to be Canadian built! Graveley and Mepal also survived, earmarked as transport aircraft bases.

Evidence of Beccles of the past remains, of a station with the usual 2,000 and two 1,500 yd runways, two 'T2' hangars and

50 loop hardstandings. But active Beccles is quite a different affair. North Sea oil was barely flowing when *Action Stations 1* appeared, whereas North Sea Gas has been extracted over many years. British Airways' helicopter operations from Beccles have increased using a variety of aircraft types—Sikorsky S-61s and S-76s and Westland WG 30s participating in North Sea energy developments. Similar flights are also taken from Bristow's Heliport at North Denes, Great Yarmouth, *(TG520106)*, which also has two short grass runways, and also from the Bacton North Sea Gas Terminal in Norfolk.

Bekesbourne, Kent (IX)

The basic equipment of No 50 Squadron can now be confirmed as BE 2/BE 12 variants plus a few of the unwieldy FK 8s—until about May 1918 when SE 5As were received. Largely because of the time taken to warm up their liquid-cooled Hispano Suiza engines before take-off, these powerful scouts did not prove successful as interceptors. They were therefore replaced by rotary-engined Sopwith Camels during August and these remained in use until disbandment in 1919.

Belfast Harbour (Sydenham), Down

See Sydenham.

Benbecula, Western Isles (VII)

Used by British Airways and Loganair, serving Glasgow and Barra.

Common sight of the 1980s, as a pair of Fairchild A-10s approach an East Anglian airfield.

Benson, Oxfordshire (VI)

SU627914.

Benson, a permanent station, remains a smaller airfield than many. By the end of the war it boasted two concrete and tar runways with wood chip topping, 069/249 of 1,990 yd and 020/200 of 1,420 yd, with its hangars amounting to four Type 'C', three Over Blister and four Extra Over Blisters. It had ten 120-ft-diameter concrete hardstandings. Now it has one active runway, 01/19 of 5,981 ft.

It remains the base of the Queen's Flight its Andovers now replaced by BAe 146s, and is also the home of the seven red and white Andover E3/3As of No 115 Squadron, which moved in from Brize Norton in January 1983. These are used for radar calibration duty, and have a secondary role as casualty evacuation air-

On the ground that daily monstrosity, the A-10, is just as ugly as it is in the air.

craft. Before taking up residence at Aldergrove in 1983 the Wessex helicopters of 72 Squadron briefly used Benson.

Bentwaters, Suffolk (I)

In 1979 grey camouflaged Fairchild A-10 Thunderbolt IIs were arriving at Bentwaters, the first squadron to commence re-equipping, in January 1979, being the 92nd. The 78th Squadron at Woodbridge starting converting in May and the 91st in July 1979. April 1979 saw the first elements operational and by September 1980 the 81st Tactical Fighter Wing, now expanded to six squadrons by the addition of Nos 509, 510 and 511, was operational. Since that time many Hardened Aircraft Shelters, themselves very much a 1980s feature, have been erected here to accommodate some of the now dreary green 120 A-10s operated by the 81st Tactical Fighter Wing. Four squadrons of A-10As, Nos 92, 509, 510 and 511 Tactical Fighter Squadrons, are now based at Bentwaters, many of whose aircraft spend time at Forward Operations Locations at Sembach, Leipheim, Ahlhorn and Norvenich in Germany. Each detachment employs about eight of over 100 A-10As available. From the high Scottish hills to the low East Anglian heights, by way of the Welsh Mountains and The Wash, the single-seater A-10s have become very much a part of our lives. They may be a shorter-lived sight than originally intended, so maybe aircraft enthusiasts should not ignore them as 'so uninteresting', as seems so often to be the case!

Bicester, Oxfordshire (VI)

Gliding still takes place from Bicester. The one-time married quarters have been sold for civilian use, likewise the sumptuous Officers' mess, now known as Cherwell College. When you pass Bicester notice its pristine Guard House, a most imperious portal, still.

Biggin Hill, Kent (VIII)

Biggin Hill Airport has two hard surface runways, Runway 21/03, 2,000 × 50 yd, and Runway 29/11, 885 × 30 yd. Lighting on Runway 21/03 is Category L3 and VASIs are positioned on Runway 21 which is the instrument runway. With its new extended terminal building, Biggin Hill is geared to the requirements of the modern flying businessman and visiting pilots. There is a new fuel installation and landing fees are low by comparison with other airports with similar facilities in the London area.

Binbrook, Lincolnshire (II)

The airfield still houses the only remaining Lightning jet fighters in service with the Royal Air Force. They are with Nos 5 and 11 Squadrons and the Lightning Training Flight (LTF). Although the Lightning is rather old in the tooth, a major refitting programme got underway in June 1985. Modifications for strengthening the wing roots on the ageing fighters were being carried out at Royal Air Force Binbrook by base engineers and civilian colleagues from British Aerospace. In charge of the programme was Squadron Leader Ray Smith who said that the refurbished Lightnings would be able to soldier on until at least 1987. They are still there.

When the Lightnings finally go from Binbrook the fate of the airfield is un-

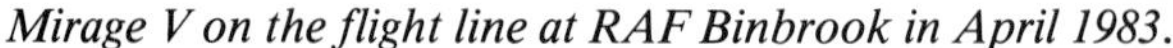

Mirage V on the flight line at RAF Binbrook in April 1983.

Above *Close up of Wing Commander Mike Streten's — (Red Dog) Officer Commanding No 5 Squadron — Lightning and of the Shark Mouth which he had painted on while in Cyprus.*

Below *A wet and windy day on the flight line at RAF Binbrook. No 5 Squadron Lightnings just back from the sun in Cyprus, two of them displaying the 'Shark's Mouth'.*

Bottom *A memorial for 460 Squadron, Royal Australian Air Force, on the roadside at the entrance to Binbrook village.*

certain. The Army has shown an interest and the Americans have paid the station a visit. How nice it would be if the old wartime airfield could be retained as a working museum. Move in the Battle of Britain Flight from Coningsby, the Vulcan from Waddington and as each aircraft becomes redundant (the next being the Jet Provost), retain one in flying condition at Binbrook. The ATC could use the airfield for summer camp and the airshows would preserve the airfield and aircraft for future generations.

Birch, Essex (I)

O/S ref T/C. 5 miles SW of Colchester
Birch was built in 1942-43 as a typical temporary wartime station for the US 9th AF. It had three runways, 080/260 of 2,000 yd and two of 1,400 yd—020/200 and 130/310. Two 'T2' hangars were sited here, and 50 spectacle hardstandings. Accommodation was for about 2,800 personnel.

Birch served mainly as an assembly and storage centre for USAAF gliders, both Waco CG-4As and the larger late war CG-13As. It was here, too, that Airspeed Horsa gliders passed to the Americans were held.

Bishops Court, Down (VII)

Tentatively allocated to the USAAF for bomber CCRC on February 28 1942 and confirmed April 1 1943. Surplus to requirements and never occupied by the USAAF.

Bitteswell, Leicestershire (II)

In 1982 British Aerospace closed Bitteswell with the loss of 1,000 jobs and in early 1984 the 567-acre site went on the market at £4 million. The site was offered in three lots which surround the junction of the A5 and A427 Coventry-Lutterworth road, and the whole lot was purchased by ex-Spitfire pilot Mr Douglas Arnold for more than £3 million.

Mr Arnold sold Blackbushe airfield near Camberley and part of Bitteswell aerodrome was to be used to house his collection of 30 to 40 vintage aircraft. Unfortunately, things did not move as fast as Mr Arnold would have liked and some hangars were still being used temporarily for storing grain in 1985. Mr Arnold dismissed local fears that aviation would be taking a back seat to activities such as drag racing. The area already had enough commercial airports and there were no plans to use Bitteswell for club flying. However, 1986 brought new developments and the MFI furniture group bought the old aerodrome from Mr Arnold. MFI plan to build a central distribution complex on the 560-acre site. Sadly, flying will never now take place again from the old airfield.

Blackbushe, Hants (IX)

The future of the airfield is again in the melting pot following its purchase by the British Car Auction Group during the autumn of 1984. At that time the declared intention was to build a 'large new facility' on the airfield, to enlarge the restaurant area in the terminal building, and to continue limited flying operations. By the summer of 1985 considerable construction work was taking place at the western end of the airfield while flying appeared unaffected, though little had been done to the terminal building.

Boscombe Down, Wiltshire (V)

The original aerodrome covered 333 acres and by the end of August 1918 the building programme was about 50 per cent complete. Construction of the six GS aeroplane sheds and single repair shed was continued, but it now appears that the planned move of additional TDS to Boscombe was little more than a paper exercise, and that the ample hangarage completed in 1919 was used for storage

View of Bitteswell airfield in 1985.

purposes. The station closed in 1920, probably during April.

The story of the Lorenz blind approach system development at Boscombe Down deserves some expansion. Immediately following the arrival of the A&AEE in September 1939 the Blind Approach Training & Development Unit was formed as part of the Establishment. The training element was dropped in May 1940 when it became the Beam Approach Development Unit and employed Ansons and Wellingtons. It was one of the former which was used in June to prove that intelligence assessments suggesting that the Germans had a blind bombing system based on Lorenz were correct. Its codename was *Knickebein* (crooked leg) and the BADU was soon employed on making the word more appropriate than the Germans intended by secretly 'bending' the beam. The Ansons were joined in this work by the more suitable Whitley, the unit being retitled the Wireless Interception Development Unit on October 5 before becoming No 109 Squadron at the end of the year. No 109 Squadron was dispersed in January 1942, only the Wireless Investigation Flight remaining at Boscombe Down to continue research work.

Bottisham, Cambridgeshire (I)

A recently unearthed point of interest concerning this airfield is that after the P-51s left in 1944 Bottisham was placed in Fighter Command, somewhat surprisingly as North Weald's distant satellite. For the benefit of our many American readers, the news is that little has changed in the 1980s. Huts depicted in Volume 1 remain and even the white painted posts of the main gate, on the old A45 opposite the turn to Bottisham village, are still in place.

Bourn, Cambridgeshire (I)

Wartime Bourn remains readily visible, marked by the one-time hangars of Short and Sebro and parts of runways. The conventional three were 065/245 of 1,925 yd, 007/187 of 1,600 yd and 128/308 1,400 yd long. The RAF tenants were able to make use of two 'T2' and one 'B1' hangars and 36 heavy bomber hardstandings.

In the north-eastern corner where Sebro operated, Bond Helicopters have taken over from Management Aviation and Rotorcraft still undertakes maintenance work. Among the crop-spraying Hiller 360s, Bond's red Dauphins may sometimes be seen visiting. Two Sikorsky S58Ts, the largest aircraft to call at Bourn since the war, arrived in 1980 for local storage. On the southern side of the airfield is the headquarters of the Rural Flying Corps, operator of the unusual Percival Sea Prince and a Provost which attend numerous air shows. Cessnas and other light aircraft also frequent this section of the airfield.

Bowness (Windermere), Cumbria

See Windermere.

Bradwell Bay, Essex (I)

Not until the 1960s was Bradwell finally abandoned as an airfield siting. In the closing months of its existence it served as a night fighter Forward Airfield in the North Weald Sector. Bradwell was an unusual aerodrome, with three tarmac and asphalt runways. Its 060/240 runway was of 1,890 yd, runway 120/300 of 1,400 yd and 172/352 of 1,000 yd. There were 24 protected pens each able to shelter a twin-engined night fighter and these were supplemented by 12 hardstandings. Three more large hardstandings were available for bombers needing to land at the coast. One Bellman hangar was erected at the airfield and a dozen Blister hangars. The present nuclear power station can hardly be looked upon as a widely popular feature, and recently released official documents reveal Bradwell's equal unpopularity as a potential airfield. The farmer who post-war cultivated the airfield site persistently went out of his way to produce holes and erect posts on runway lines apparently to discourage the RAF from ever returning to what was for 15 post-war years listed as a site for wartime development. Its derelict state (Category 5) discouraged plans for Bradwell to be up-dated to accommodate two Short-Range Day fighter squadrons. Had that come about, then Rivenhall would have become its standby station.

Bratton, Shropshire (III)

The FAA had several Tiger Moths here by the main entrance. There was also occasionally an Anson and an Argus by the railway station end. When the Masters came from Condover they were all parked along the northern perimeter. A Horsa force-landed when its Albemarle tug got into difficulties. During 1944 a Thunderbolt coded *VM-P* from Atcham with red nose and white rudder belly-landed on approach.

Brawdy, Dyfed (III)

No 517 Squadron moved to Chivenor on November 26 1945. In its early years as a RNAS it was a tender to, and diversion for the night fighter school at Dale. In August 1947 it was reduced to Care and Maintenance until recommissioned as a full air station in September 1952. Over the period 1951 to 1955 a large building and works programme was carried out to bring Brawdy (now HMS *Goldcrest*) up to peace-time standards. (Many of the war-time Nissen huts were in such bad condition that on at least one occasion a roof was blown off in a gale.) To enable the base to become an advanced flying training centre and also to take over the front line aircraft holding task from RNAS Abbotsinch, it was reconstructed between 1961 and '63. The improvements included three new interconnected hangars and an adjoining technical block and the addition of 500 yd to the main runway. Units present during its last years with the Navy included 738, 759 and 849 Squadrons and the Naval Aircraft Support Unit.

Brize Norton, Oxfordshire (VI)

Brize Norton remains one of Britain's most important airfields and has long been one of the largest. Indeed, by the end of the war it had two very long runways, 086/266 being of 3,000 yd and 044/224 of 2,000 yd. The wide assortment of hangars then included four Type 'C's, five 'T' Types, two 'D' Types (still boldly evident), six Lamellas, two Bellmans, two Standard Blisters, five Over Blisters, 15 Robin Blisters and one Bellman Oversize. Little wonder No 6 MU, the Aircraft Servicing Unit here, handled so many aircraft during and soon after the war.

Brian Walker wrote recalling his time with 6 MU. In 1948, he says, a line of captured German aircraft remained. Many Liberators were melted down here, on site, into metal 'bricks', the smelting being done in a mobile furnace which looked like a pitch boiler. 'It was moved from place to place wrecking as it progressed', he tells us. 'If the next aircraft to be dealt with was one of the German collection, in it went. The quest for aluminium overrode all other considerations, even though all of us were upset. We could do nothing, orders were orders. Among what seemed to be hundreds of Spitfires on the airfield could be seen insignia of French, Belgian, Polish air forces, parked in the field at the side of the Witney road where the station's main entrance now is. All went into the same pot, all to make ingots. What a shame it is

An excellent painting by John Young of Halifax Mk III, LV794, *of No 78 Squadron, bombing up at Breighton on February 25 1944, for a raid on Augsburg. A bomber force of 594 aircraft was dispatched and 21 bombers failed to return, one being* LV794. *It was shot down on the way to the target by a Ju 88 night-fighter and crashed near Dahn, Saarland. Three crew members, including the captain, Flight Lieutenant W.M. Carruthers, were killed, the other four being taken prisoner.*

Aerial view of Brough in the 1980s.

that not one of us could influence those in control into keeping at least some of these reminders of what had kept Britain free.'

Hear, hear, Mr Walker. I knew the feeling when I had to set fire to a giant pile of gliders. Please forgive me, too!

Brize Norton of the 1980s is a very different place with its 10,006 ft asphalt runway 08/26, load factor LCGII. That means that it can virtually accept the weightiest of all aircraft so it is not surprising that Brize Norton is the chosen base for the RAF's heaviest ever aircraft, the TriStars. Long the home of the VC-10s of No 10 Squadron, Brize Norton now accommodates the RAF's five VC-10 K 2 tankers and four VC-10 K 3s (Super VC-10s converted, the first entering service in February 1985) which equip 101 Squadron. The latter re-formed here on May 1 1984, and the earlier possibility that Vulcan tankers might be based here lapsed. To make way for the recent developments the Andover E 3s of 115 Squadron moved to Benson in January 1983.

No 10 Squadron's dozen VC-10s still display the roundel in many distant parts of the world, often conveying royalty and VVIPs as well. Services are also operated in particular to Cyprus and Belize, while the Ascension run will presumably be reduced. Support is also given to exercises and troop movements, and in a war situation VC-10s would serve in battle support.

Crews for the transport aircraft continue to be trained by 241 OCU which borrows aircraft as needed. When consideration was given to assessing the suitability for the Queen's Flight of the BAe 146-100, 241 OCU handled the task using *ZD695 (G-OBAF)* and *ZD696 (G-SCHH)*, both of which have returned to civilian hands. No 1 Parachute Training School is also here, responsible for training paratroopers as well as fielding the famous 'Falcons', the RAF's parachute team. JATE (the Joint Air Transport Establishment) continues to conduct trials and development of ideas for improving transport operations, and Brize Norton is now the base of No 19 Squadron, RAF Regiment, which is equipped with Rapier surface-to-air guided weapons. Its task is the defence of US bases in Britain. Thus, this is a very busy station whose activities began to take on more enormous proportions when the TriStars nosed in.

It was June 1983 when two ex-British Airways TriStars commenced trooping flights from Brize Norton, giving the station a taste of what was involved in the handling and operation of wide-bodied jets with a capacity far in advance of anything previously in Service hands. Merely taxying the newcomer around the perimeter track of some of the most sophisticated RAF airfields needs care, and the weight of the aircraft further restricts it when fairly heavily loaded. October 1983 saw RAF aircrew joining the flight crews of British Airways then on November 1 1983 216 Squadron reformed and soon applied its insignia to the tails of the TriStars. Eventually 216 Squadron will hold at least six TriStars, K1 tankers and KC1s with special cargo facilities permitting lengthy support to fighter patrols and rapid overseas reinforcements. Full-scale operations are some way off, with the TriStar having the potential to be useful well into the next century.

Brockton, Shropshire (III)

A Robin hangar still stands on the northern boundary. Bar and rod tracking was used for hardstandings and many fences are constructed from it.

Bruntingthorpe, Leicestershire (II)

After many secret meetings a group of businessmen and aviation enthusiasts made it known in September 1985 that Bruntingthorpe airfield could become Europe's largest aviation museum for the wealthy Walton family, who own the airfield, planned to give it to the Confederate Air Force which has its base in Texas. Bruntingthorpe could thus have become the European Headquarters for the Confederate Air Force and the French wing of the CAF announced it was to back the project. In the end, however, Bruntingthorpe was passed over by the CAF who chose Coventry instead.

Brunton, Northumberland (VII)

The runways and perimeter track are in excellent condition and public access is permitted *provided* one does not enter any of the runways. These are used by parachuting and other private aircraft. All the buildings have been cleared apart from some of the blast shelters.

Bude, Cornwall

SS238013. 4 miles SSE of Bude off minor road.

The large airship station at Mullion spawned a number of mooring-out sites during 1918, partially to provide alternative refuge when bad weather closed the main base, but also to cut down on transit time to the operating areas. The latter was a particular problem for airships working off the north Cornwall coast and so it was decided to locate one of the sub-stations near Bude. A heavily wooded valley near the hamlet of Langford Barton was chosen. Sheltered from the prevailing south-westerlies it had the added advantage of being close to metalled roads and the railway line connecting Bude to the rest of the country.

Below *Me108 at Bruntingthorpe*

Bottom *Old wartime Nissen huts at Bruntingthorpe.*

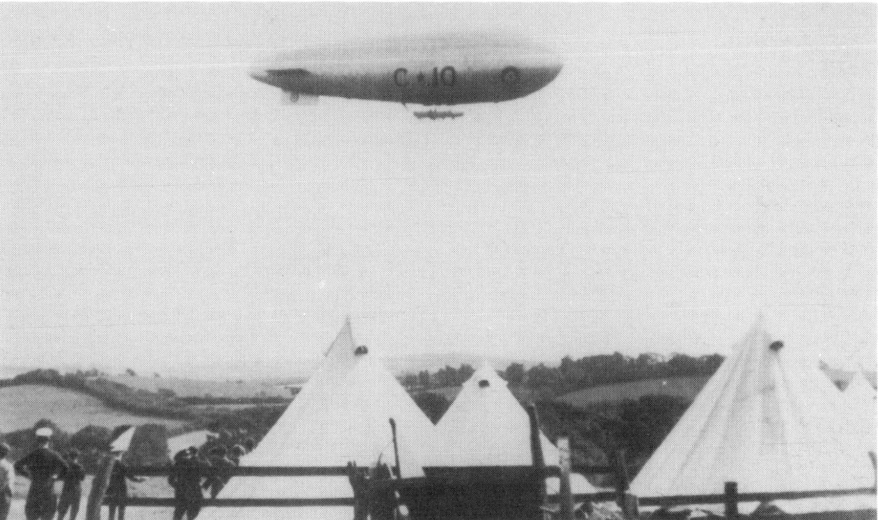

Top *Wartime watch office at Bruntingthorpe as at June 1984.*

Above *The coastal non-rigid airship* 10 *powered by its 240 hp Fiat and 110 hp Berliet engines overflies the Bude mooring-out site in 1918. The tents of Naval ratings dominate the foreground with the wooded valley mooring site visible behind* (Osborne Studios).

Handling crews were detached from RNAS Mullion and initially lived in tents while the officers were quartered in the requisitioned Langford Barton House. The site was capable of accommodating two Coastal-type airships moored to large concrete blocks and kept fully inflated. All maintenance except minor daily servicing was done at Mullion.

Operational patrols were carried out over the St George's and Bristol Channels under the control of the C-in-C Devonport. By October 1918 the unit was part of No 9 Group, RAF, and flying continued until the end of the year, the *SSZ 75* being 'diverted' to Padstow late in December because gale force winds made it impossible to haul down the 'ship' in the confined space available at Bude.

The decision early in 1919 to cease non-rigid airship operations resulted in a rapid run-down and Bude sub-station was soon abandoned. The wooden huts which had replaced tents during the previous autumn were then used for agricultural purposes for some years. Nothing obvious now remains though a thorough search of the woods might reveal some of the concrete mooring blocks—such objects are notoriously long-lived.

Burnaston, Derbyshire (II & III)

Considered in 1942 for possible development as a bomber OTU but the existing EFTS had greater priority at that time so it remained a grass aerodrome. No 49 Gliding School formed here by June 1945, moving to Castle Donington in spring 1946. The airfield re-opened for private flying in July 1987.

Burscough, Lancashire (III)

The tower was refurbished in 1981 by a parachuting club but by 1983 operations had been suspended. The radio beacon was removed about the same time. Private flying re-started on a limited basis in 1985.

Burtonwood, Cheshire (III)

No 635 Gliding School moved to Samlesbury in October 1983. The three 'C' Type hangars were demolished in 1985. A Dome Trainer can be seen near the tower. The first of Burtonwood's three towers, a pre-war 'Fort' type, was probably removed when the apron was extended after the war.

Calshot, Hants (V)

SU489025.

The final paragraph of the *Action Stations 5* entry was prophetic—for a couple of years prior to its enforced removal to Chatham in November 1984 Sunderland V *G-BJHS (ML814/NZ4108)* was undergoing restoration behind 'F' Shed at Calshot! Like 'G' Shed, this timber-framed, corrugated iron-clad hangar was built in 1917, and with the steel-framed 'H' Shed makes up most of the present-day accommodation of the Activities Centre.

Levelling the ground for the 'H' Shed was well in hand during the summer of 1918 and it was completed the following year with three sets of side opening doors down its 625 ft long west side. This enormous building is 120 ft wide and is

Below *Marathon* G-AMHR *of Derby Airways at Burnaston on July 26 1960.*

Bottom *1772 Squadron crew with Firefly* Z1946 *at Burscough, summer 1944* (V.M.G. Bennett).

Top *Razorback Thunderbolts awaiting collection at Burtonwood in 1943. The 'C' Type hangars have now been demolished along with the original 'fort' type tower in front* (via A.P. Ferguson).

Above *Oxford* T1341/R2 *of No 11 PAFU, Calveley, over the Cheshire Plain in 1944.*

perfect for indoor sports, the facilities even including a ski run trainer. For some strange reason the sheds have now been dazzle painted in combinations of white, brown, light and dark green, but the original lecture block (now used for student accommodation) is more decorously adorned with a large Schneider Trophy seaplane mural on its south-facing exterior wall.

The Officer's Mess, believed to have been built in 1914, is now an inn rejoicing in the name, 'The Flying Boat'. The walls of the lounge are covered in photographs and paintings of seaplanes, flying boats and Calshot personnel. It's worth a visit for this reason alone, but the beer is good as well!

Calveley, Cheshire (III)

A good example of a 'Seagull Trench' defence structure stands on a hillock near to the tower.

Cambridge (Teversham), Cambridgeshire (I)

TL487586. By Newmarket Road leading easterly out of Cambridge.

Cambridge remains one of the most interesting aerodromes in the area. It is privately owned by Marshall of Cambridge (Engineering), Ltd, which runs its own flying school whose three Cessna 150s after 20 years service were changed for '152s in September 1983. Cambridge is the base for the Pembroke Dock Taxi Company, the Chipmunks of No 5 Air Experience Flight and also the four Bulldogs of the Cambridge University Air Squadron. Although the then-unusual Short SD 3-30 of Inter-City Airlines ceased operations mid-season, on July 29 1983, others took over the Channel Islands' run and Cambridge continues to serve as a terminal for holiday flights by Viscounts of British Air Ferries to Guernsey and Jersey under arrangement with Premier Airlines whose services

Memorable indeed was the arrival at Cambridge in August 1968 of aircraft setting off to complete the filming of The Battle of Britain *in the south of France.*

attract around 15,000 passengers each summer season.

Regular flights in support of Cambridge electronics factories are made by the Dassault Falcon and Beech KingAir of the Philips Flight, based at Eindhoven. Horse traffic connected with Newmarket continues, conveyance to Ireland and the Continent being by Aer Turas CL-44 and uncommonly by Argosy or Vanguard, while wealthy horse owners arrive at Cambridge in their private jets before heading for race meetings. Cambridge University Gliding Club has its base here, but flying takes place from Duxford. The Cambridge Private Flying Group still flies two beautifully maintained Tiger Moths, the very special and aged *G-AHIZ* and *G-AOEI*, plus more modern light aircraft.

Marshall is respected world-wide for its extremely high quality workmanship, frequently applied during modification and overhaul of Lockheed and Gulfstream products, and in support of the Cessna Citation executive jet in Europe. Periodically other aircraft types come here for maintenance including 'privately owned' Boeing 727s. A steady flow of Gulfstream 1s, 2s and 3s call for attention, owned by wealthy individuals, governments and companies. To particularly cope with this specialised trade, Marshall had a large

Below *Unique to 5 AEF and Cambridge, the Beagle Husky* XW635.

Bottom *Worth a bit! Two RAF Tristars by the large new Cambridge hangar,* ZD950 *the trials aircraft nearest and* ZD953, *first service tanker, behind.*

hangar erected in 1980.

The company probably remains best known, though, for its over 20-year support programme for the RAF's Lockheed Hercules fleet. Updating of radio and navigation aids, formation lights, general structural maintenance and repainting are all typical of the tasks undertaken. Completed in November 1985 was the contract covering insertion of two sections into the fuselages of 29 aircraft. Lengthening them thus has produced the RAF's Hercules 3s, some of which in 1984-85, along with a few Mk 1s acquired overall grey-green camouflage in the process. Marshall has also overhauled C-130s for civilian operators and for the Royal Swedish and Danish Air Forces among others.

Long remembered will be the Marshall 24-hour seven-day superb marathon effort over six weeks in 1982 to produce Hercules in-flight refuellers and tankers for the establishment of an air bridge to the Falklands. On April 16 1982 Marshall was asked to equip a Hercules 1 for in-flight refuelling; in less than a fortnight *XV200*, the trials example, was flying and on May 5 was returned, ready, to the RAF. Within another week probed *XV179* was also flying. The increased range given to the Hercules permitted special mail and even personnel to be parachuted to forces in the South Atlantic area. By means of a towed grappling hook, urgently required items could be snatched from the sea and land.

That achieved, the company was on April 30 asked to produce a Hercules tanker to supplement Marham's much overworked Victors, and another Mk 1, *XV296*, became the first of six Hercules tankers. Packed into its fuselage were huge fuel tanks, from which a transfer hose was led through a rear floor, box-like arrangement into which was built a series of lights to guide the pilot of the refuelling aircraft. The Hercules maintained the only frequent air transport link between Ascension and the Falklands until Mount Pleasant airfield opened in 1985. For some who undertook the 12-hour flight from Ascension in a Hercules there were uneasy moments, the strong wind frequently sweeping Port Stanley making landing hazardous, even impossible. Skill and an ample supply of good fortune meant that not one aircraft was lost during these flights, a wonderful tribute to all concerned.

The Falklands' conflict highlighted the inadequacy of the British tanker fleet. Although the Victors did well, they were ageing and intensive flying could only hasten their end. Conversion of ex-civil VC-10s was undertaken at Filton and, doubtless impressed by the capabilities of the USAAF transport/tanker KC-10 Extender, the Air Staff decided that Britain must possess aircraft with similar reinforcement capability. Although the McDonnell DC-10 was available, indeed was demonstrated to the British during the 1982 SBAC Display period, its cost was high. Instead, British Airways was able to release some overcapacity by way of TriStars, which were seemingly cheaper to acquire.

Marshall, with its tanker and Falklands' experience, won the contract to undertake the necessary modifications of TriStars. To the end of the contract battle the company had been on tenterhooks. As soon as it was won Boulton & Paul of Norwich erected the steel frame of a giant hangar forming the South Works, one of Europe's largest buildings and able to house as many as five TriStars.

On February 16 1983 the first TriStar 500 arrived, long before the hangar was complete. So massive and powerful was the aircraft that traffic lights were installed on roads near the 06/24 6,446 ft concrete runway ends to safeguard high sided vehicles in the area. Return to service of several unmodified TriStars has since come about mainly because the modification programme proved more complicated than originally envisaged,

At least two civilian Chipmunks are flying in Cambridge University Air Squadron colours. This, though, is an original in the first 'block style' dayglo trim.

much due to differences between each TriStar.

The TriStars are the heaviest aircraft the RAF has ever operated, the tankers having an all-up weight of well over 500,000 lb, and that of course precludes the aircraft from flying from Cambridge other than in lightly loaded state. *ZD950*, the first to be converted and which had entered the hangar for the task on August 10 1983, undertook its initial flight early on July 9 1985 just in time for a public airing at the Fairford Air Tattoo. It was delivered to Boscombe Down for trials starting late in 1985. The second TriStar K1, *ZD953*, first flew on December 23 1985. Early machines may eventually return for additional air-air refuelling pods beneath the wings so that the TriStar looks set to be a Cambridge sight for a long time to come. The possibility that civilian TriStar operators will also make use of Marshall's new skills was shown when late 1985 saw internal modifications made to two TriStars of Worldways, Canada.

Campbeltown, Strathclyde (VII)

The pre-war aerodrome here was known as 'The Strath' and the hangar and some of the huts dating from World War 2 were still in existence at Dalivaddy Farm in 1970 and probably still are.

Cardiff (Pengam Moors), South Glamorgan

See Pengam Moors.

Cark, Cumbria (III)

First used from April 1939 by 'B' Flight, 1 AACU, with Henley target tugs. Cark was also HQ of 6 AACU from March 15 1942 until March 12 1943. No 188 Gliding School formed here by February 1944 and moved to Barrow early in 1947.

Castle Archdale, Lough Erne (VII)

The last operational sortie by a Coastal Command aircraft from here was on June 3/4 1945 by Sunderland *'Z'* of 201 Squadron to escort an eastbound convoy.

Castle Donington, Leicestershire (II)

East Midlands International Airport (ex-Castle Donington), continues to make progress and the airlines using the airport at the time of writing were Air-Bridge Carriers; Aer Lingus; British Midland

G-BECE, *Airship* AD500 *flying over Cardington in 1979.*

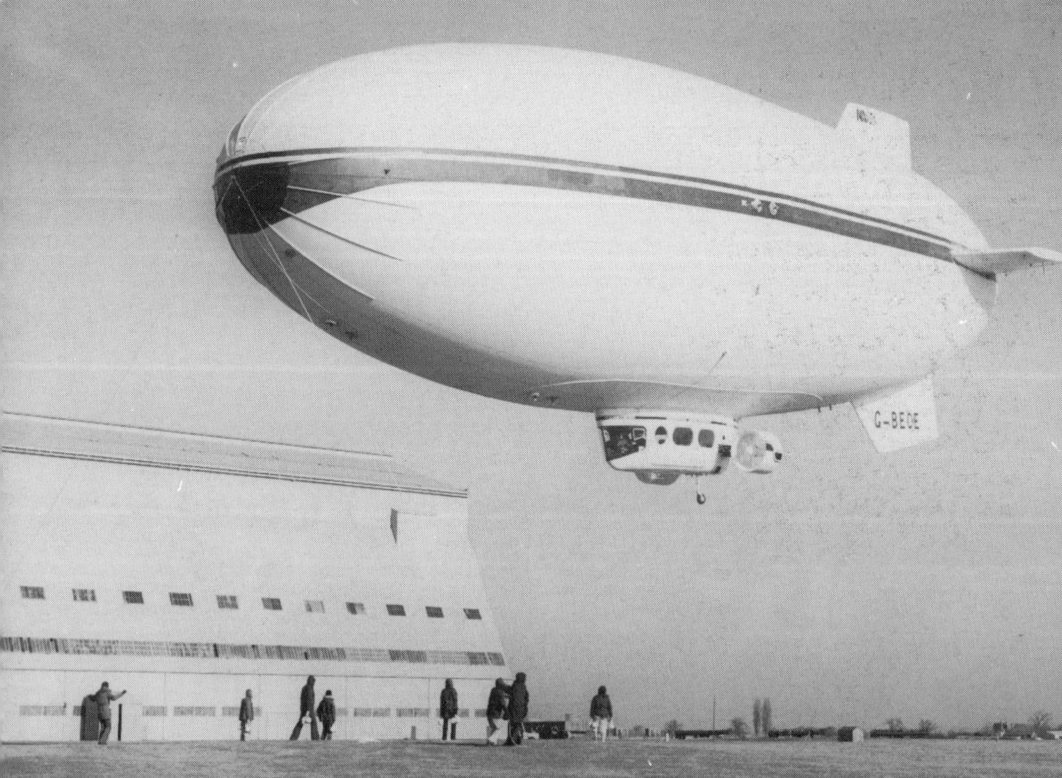

Above *Maintenance area at Castle Archdale. Note operation block bottom right with massive concrete slab over control room* (P.H.T. Green Collection). **Below** *Remains of a wartime dispersal pan at Castle Donington (now East Midlands Airport) in June 1984.* **Bottom** *An Orion Boeing 737-300 high in the clouds heading towards the sun.*

The Boeing 737 flight simulator in operation at East Midlands International Airport.

Airways; Britannia Airways; Brymon Airways; Dan Air Services; Elan Air; Euroflite, and Orion Airways who operate the super-quiet Boeing 737-300.

Orion decided to purchase four Boeing 737-300 SQs and, finding the training facilities for it inadequate, they invested £5 million in a Boeing 737-300 flight simulator, the only one of its kind in the world. The Rediffusion Flight Simulator is housed in a purpose-built building at the Orion HQ at East Midlands International Airport. Pilots now come to Castle Donington from all over the world (including some from Boeing) to use Orion's flight simulator. The simulator module, which took over 18 months to build, has six subtle movements, using hydraulic pistons, and the computer is capable of 3.7 million instructions per second. The computer can come up with any weather conditions, even rare examples of clear-air turbulence or emergency such as a mid-air collision. This means pilots can be trained to full operational standards whilst the aircraft themselves remain available for normal passenger service.

East Midlands International Airport has direct scheduled air services to the UK's major cities and to a number of key European cities. There are frequent commuter services to Heathrow and Schipol airports for onward connections to all parts of the world. For holidaymakers it is the gateway to the sun, Majorca, Cyprus, Spain, Portugal, Greece, Bulgaria, the Canary Islands, North Africa, Italy and

Vickers Merchantman G-APES, *formerly a BEA Vanguard, seen here at East Midlands International Airport in 1984.*

Malta. During the period from 1979, when *Action Stations 2* was published, to 1984, East Midlands International Airport was the United Kingdom's fastest growing major airport. From April 1 1984 to March 31 1985 passenger throughput was up by 9.7 per cent to 1,071,760.

On the air freight side, business also continued to expand dramatically, the main companies being Air Express International; Elan International; Express Air Freight; LEP Transport; Midlands Import-Export Services; Pan Am; Pandair Freight; RH Freight, and TNT Transcontinental Freight. Another important factor for the future of the airport is its position. It is very conveniently situated within a network of A roads and motorways—M1, M5, M6 and M42—which are still being further developed.

Therefore, the future of East Midlands International Airport looks set to continue and in 1985 was still being surged forwards by the driving force of Mr Eric Dyer, the General Manager. However, the multi-million pound runway extension, which could create up to 2,500 badly needed jobs, has been postponed for 'the foreseeable future' by the Labour-controlled administration. One shudders to think what the outcome of the war might have been with such narrow-minded people at the helm.

Castletown, Highland (VII)

The story of how an RAF station acquired and lost a large calibre naval gun is quite amusing. Apparently, a naval vessel went aground and was pounded on the rocks until it was a total loss. Aerial reconnaissance, however, indicated the survival of a large gun fitted on the stern. An RAF party equipped with cutting gear removed it with great difficulty, together with whatever ammunition could be salvaged, and thus complemented the almost non-existent ground-to-air defences of RAF Castletown. It was mounted in concrete outside the Station HQ which unfortunately removed its ability to move in a horizontal plane. Even more unfortunate was the fact that its over-rigid emplacement left it pointing directly at the local lighthouse, to the alarm of the occupants!

Parties of amateur artillerymen practised discharging the piece until Atcherley, the CO, overplayed his hand by indenting to the Admiralty for a fresh supply of ammunition when the first batch was exhausted. In a matter of days a band of indignant sailors arrived to retrieve the weapon and Castletown once again lay wide open to enemy air attack.

Charlton Horethorne, Somerset (V)

No 790 Squadron actually re-formed at Charlton Horethorne on July 27 1942 equipped with Oxfords (which represented bombers) and Fulmars (fighters) for use as targets for the Air Direction School. These two types of aircraft soldiered on until June 1944 when the weary Fulmars were replaced by Fireflies—the only other type used by the squadron whilst at Charlton Horethorne.

The correct title of 765 Squadron was the Travelling Recording Unit and, because Charlton Horethorne was not suitable for the Wellingtons used by the unit, it is probable that association with the station was confined to initial formation in March 1944. Certainly the Wellingtons were nominally based at Lee-on-Solent though they actually flew from other airfields as detached Flights until moving to Malta during November 1945.

Many of the original fighter pens to the west of the Blackford-Corton Denham road do still exist, as do some of the huts on the edge of the west facing escarpment. It should be noted, however, that they are on private property, not accessible without permission.

Charmy Down, Somerset (V)

The Americans not only used Charmy Down (Station 487) as the 4th Tactical Air Depot from November 1943 but also as temporary accommodation for a couple of very unhappy night fighter squadrons.

Assigned to the 9th Tactical Air Command of the 9th Air Force, the personnel of the 422nd Night Fighter Squadron, USAAF, crossed the Atlantic aboard the SS *Mauretania*. They reached Charmy Down on March 7 1944 with instructions to settle in and await arrival of their mighty P-61 Black Widow twin-boom fighters and found the tail end of the English winter a sore trial. The squadron diarist recorded Charmy Down as 'on the windiest hill top in all southern England' and 'our suffering comparable to Washington's men at Valley Forge until we learnt how to keep coke burning'.

The 9th AF was not involved in night operations and thus had no interest in the 'black art' of night fighting, or the fate of

The Officers' Mess at Chivenor—one of the many new buildings on this largely rebuilt RAF station.

the squadron. The P-61s were delayed and with their only equipment an Oxford and a Cessna Bobcat the squadron got no worthwhile training until they moved to Scorton on May 7. They were replaced on May 26 by the other 9th AF P-61 unit, the 425th, but they too moved on to Scorton, leaving Charmy Down on June 12 1944—and with no regrets!

Charterhall, Borders (VII)

The decontamination centre exists on the old Officers' Mess site.

Chedburgh, Suffolk (I)

There is nothing more galling than to read a book and feel that it has not done justice to a particular feature. But space is always at a premium and often the author has to decide 'what do I leave out?' Flight Lieutenant A.T. Gable quite rightly felt that both 214 and 620 Squadrons had received less than their fair share in Volume 1. He wrote: 'The casual mention of those squadrons makes it appear as if they were being rested! Missions in their aircraft and from those squadrons were very nearly suicidal.

'As a crew we made our first flight with 620 Squadron on June 21 1943 and our last on November 4. In that time our losses were so bad that the beds in our dispersed living accommodation became unoccupied and re-occupied so rapidly that we just did not get time to know anyone and no crews were becoming "tour experienced". Our crew was finally made such after 28 operations, together with another crew which flew 27, the only crews to complete tours in five months. In that time we had visited such places as Gelsenkirchen, Cologne, Hamburg four times, Essen, Remscheid, Nuremburg twice, Italy twice, Peenemünde, Berlin twice, Münchengladbach, Kassel, Bremen and flew numerous mining operations to Biscay, the Frisians and the Kattegat.

'We made, perhaps, one of the first sighting reports of jet night fighters (confirmed many years later by meeting the ex-Luftwaffe pilot concerned and matching log book details). As a crew we were awarded three DFCs and three DFMs.'

So, when next you pass what remains of Chedburgh, perhaps you will recall its Stirling days and just what ghastly things overtook many who set forth from the Suffolk airfield. For myself, I never cross the Alps without marvelling how anyone had the courage to make such a crossing in total darkness, between the peaks, in a Wimpey or a Stirling. It took a long, frightening time then; now it is a non-event taking but a few moments. On a dark night—or even in treacherous icy moonlight—you had to be very brave.

Chetwynd, Shropshire (III)

Not used 1950 to 1961 as unsuitable for Provost aircraft, retained in reserve.

Childs Ercall (Peplow), Shropshire

See Peplow.

Chivenor, Devon (V)

A remarkable collection of wartime memorabilia is now on display at RAF Chivenor. Named the 'Pat Knight Collection', it is the result of one man's single-minded determination to build up a selection of artefacts representative of aviation in North Devon—achieved despite constant ill-health. It is on view in the main briefing room of the Operations Block—a constant source of interest to the students passing through No 2 TWU. Unfortunately the collection cannot be viewed by the general public except by special arrangement.

The annual open day was reinstated in 1984 and provides a wonderful opportunity to visit the station (usually in July) and see the many fine new buildings and the Hawks. Many of the latter are now capable of operations as air defence fighters and look very striking in their light grey colour scheme. The main rebuilding programme came to an end in 1985, one of the last of the smart dark red brick buildings to be completed being the new-style air traffic control, positioned so that controllers will be able to monitor all parts of the airfield for the first time since the re-opening in August 1980.

Church Broughton, Derbyshire (III)

The correct title for the 93 Group Instructors' Pool was the 93 Group Screened Pilots School. Mr E. Walker, a staff pilot with the school, has provided further information as no official records appear to have survived. It was formed in May 1943 in an effort to reduce the fatal accident rate at bomber OTUs which was causing so much concern. Almost all the instructors at OTUs were aircrew who had completed one or more operational tours with Bomber Command and were for a period 'screened' from further operations. Since places on FIS courses were scarce, few had any formal training in instructional techniques, and the 93 Group School was an effort to improve matters, unique in the three OTU Groups. It had no aircraft of its own but drew them from each of the five OTUs in the Group.

The school was disbanded in October 1944 having trained about 550 students. No 93 Group HQ evidently thought highly of the results as the six staff pilots, including the then Flight Lieutenant Walker, were all awarded the AFC.

A P-80 Shooting Star and the Trent-Meteor were often seen flying from here in 1945. A visit in 1946 revealed the presence of Vampire I *TG276*, Meteor IIIs *EE314* and *EE339/6* and Spitfire XIV *TX980*. Close by at Marchington was an 8th Air Force Supply Depot with an airstrip for light liaison aircraft.

Cluntoe, Tyrone (VII)

The additional hardstandings at this and other USAAF stations in Northern Ireland were in fact to accommodate the large numbers of aircraft expected for modification at Langford Lodge following the decision by 8th Air Force Service Command, on June 18 1943, to delegate Langford with technical responsibility for modification of all aircraft in the European Theatre, effective June 25. To that end, the CO at Langford was instructed to 'establish liaison with Burtonwood and Warton and such other stations in the Service Command as necessary to ensure that modification is promptly and properly performed on all incoming aircraft'.

Coltishall, Norfolk (I)

TG267228.

When *Action Stations 1* appeared Coltishall had fairly recently received Jaguars which remain here with Nos 6, 41 and 54 Squadrons. The main difference has concerned its air-sea rescue helicopters. Whirlwind HAR 10s of 202 Squadron were replaced by Wessex HC 2s in 'F' Flight, 22 Squadron, these being removed in favour of longer-range Sea King HAR 3s in 1981. Come the Falklands' conflict and the Sea Kings were withdrawn for use in the campaign and its aftermath, which meant the return of the Wessex. Not until 1985 did two Sea Kings of 'C' Flight, 202 Squadron, resume duty at Coltishall.

Some details of Coltishall's earlier post-war days have been lately revealed. The main runway was completed in August 1950 allowing the 24 Mosquitoes of Nos 23, 141 and 264 Squadrons to return from Church Fenton to one of the first two fighter stations to have an ASP (Aircraft Servicing Platform). Over the next few years Foulsham was prescribed as Coltishall's standby airfield, which explains that airfield's long survivability.

Condover, Shropshire (III)

First used May 15 1942 to July 30 1942 as a RLG for 5 FTS. The original single-storey watch office still stands next to the later tower. The Battle HQ is situated in a copse on the opposite side of the aerodrome. Surviving sections of the undulating runways and perimeter track are often used by crop-spraying aircraft.

Piper Pawnee G-BFRX *parked on the perimeter track at Condover in March 1982.*

Top *Original small watch office at Condover.*

Above *Tornado F 2* ZD906 *of 228 OCU taxies by at Coningsby in June 1985.*

Below *Tornado F 2* ZD934 *at RAF Coningsby.*

Coningsby, Lincolnshire (II)

In July 1985 the units at Royal Air Force Coningsby were No 228 Operational Conversion Unit and No 29 Squadron with F4 Phantoms, both units situated on the south side of the airfield in hardened accommodation. They share the airfield with No 229 Operational Conversion Unit's Tornado F2s and the Battle of Britain Memorial Flight.

The high technology Tornado F2/F3, carrying a whole new generation of radar, will replace the Phantom which has been the backbone of Coningsby for nearly 20 years. By the end of 1985 there were 16 Tornado F2s on duty at Coningsby, which will remain a Tornado airfield for the foreseeable future.

Connel, Strathclyde (VII)

In 1940 it was noted that vital areas in western Scotland, including the Naval ports at Loch Ewe and Kyle of Lochalsh and the British Aluminium works at Fort William, needed defence against air attack. Several airfields in the Western Isles were suggested as sector stations and Tiree was the eventual choice. A forward aerodrome was required on the mainland but a survey soon showed that the only possible site was on a pre-war civil landing ground at Connel. This was considered barely acceptable because of the bad approaches to the north.

Intensive glider flying now takes place here with winch launching. The site is used as an advanced base for RAF rescue

Top *Chipmunk of the Battle of Britain Memorial Flight outside the Flight's hangar at Coningsby.*

Above *Inside the Battle of Britain hangar in July 1985. Spitfire V* AB910 (*page 112,* Action Stations 2) *seen here in a new coat of paint.*

Below *The old and the new. Pictured at RAF Coningsby, the Lancaster soars high above one of the RAF's new Tornados* (Lincolnshire Echo).

Tornados show off their colours — I-40 *Italian,* G-73 *German,* B-55 *British.*

helicopters and a prominently marked fuel dump is maintained for this purpose. One of the few original buildings is the operations block now refurbished for the Royal Observer Corps.

Cottesmore, Leicestershire (II)

In January 1981 a plaque was unveiled at Royal Air Force Cottesmore by four Chiefs of Staff to mark the official opening of the Trinational Tornado Training Establishment which trains air crews of Britain, Germany and Italy. The ceremony took place in 'A' Hangar where three Tornado aircraft—one from each nation—were on display. A total of 11 aircraft stood on the tarmac for the Chiefs of Staff to inspect.

Since then the Tornados have rolled off the production line and in August 1985, the Tornados from 36 Stormo (Wing) of the Italian Air Force Base at Giola Del Colle, near Bari in Southern Italy, returned to say thank you to the people of Leicestershire with a dazzling display.

Cowdray Park, Sussex (IX)

In addition to the possible use of Cowdray park by W/T trainer Proctors (still unconfirmed), the LG hosted a number of Ansons for six months during 1944. These aircraft flew for the RN School of Photography and normally operated from Ford, but with ever-increasing congestion as the build-up for the Normandy invasion accelerated, the naval Ansons were detached to Cowdray Park. They arrived during April and operated under the auspices of the RN Storage Section until returning to Ford in October 1944.

Crail, Fife (VII)

The original small watch tower still exists. The TAT or Torpedo Attack Trainer consisted of a large and dimly lit sphere, in the centre of which was the cockpit section of a Barracuda. The image of a target ship was projected on the wall. Its function was to train TBR pilots to use the 'F Director' system of torpedo attack. It was a very good training aid and was quite advanced for that time.

Cranage, Cheshire (III)

One of the few remaining structures is the Battle HQ by the wood on the south-west perimeter. Cranage was also used by Tern Hill aircraft from July to September 1940. No 190 Gliding School formed here by May 1945 and moved to Woodvale early in 1947.

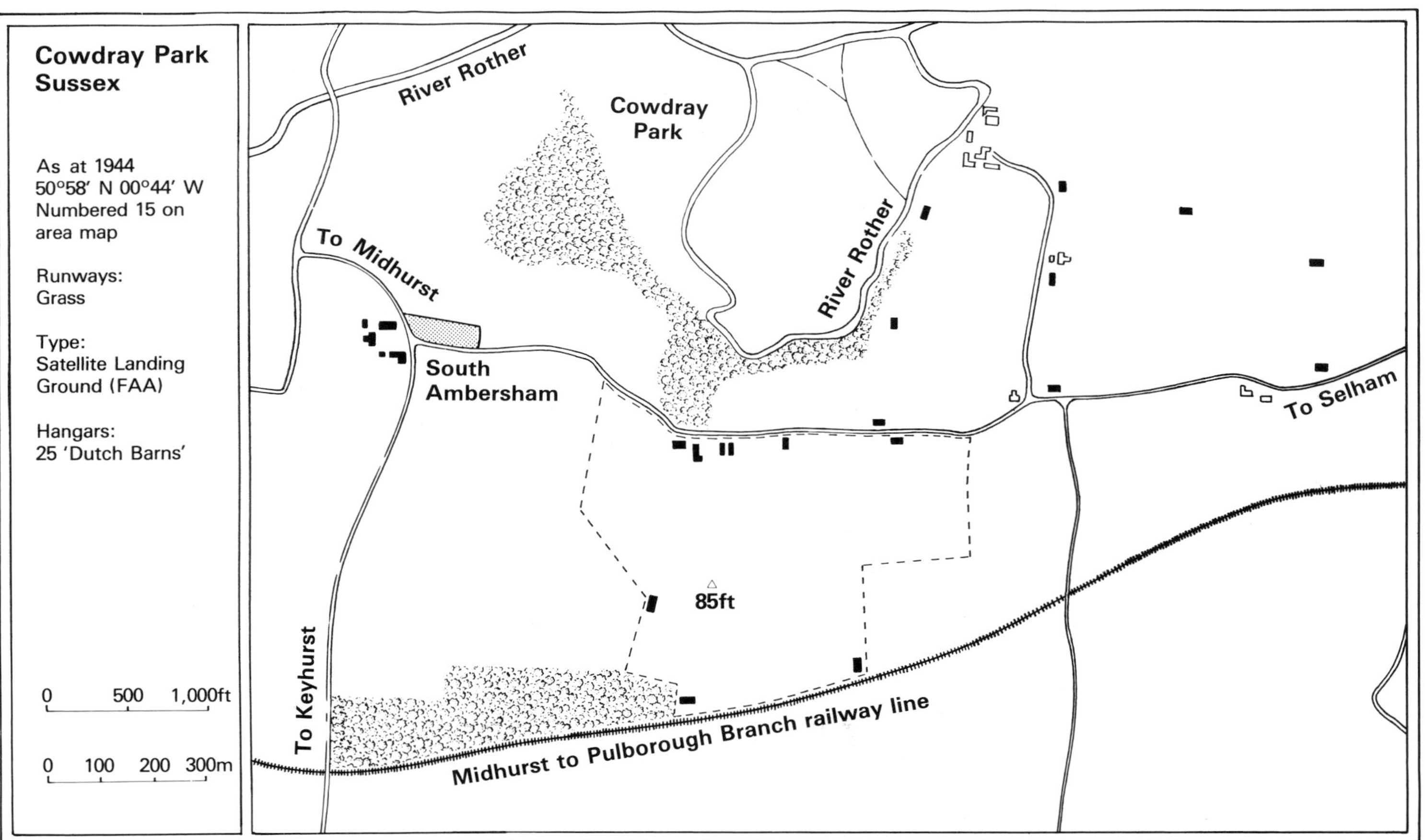
Cowdray Park
Sussex
As at 1944
50°58′ N 00°44′ W
Numbered 15 on area map
Runways:
Grass
Type:
Satellite Landing Ground (FAA)
Hangars:
25 'Dutch Barns'
0 500 1,000ft
0 100 200 300m
River Rother
Cowdray Park
To Midhurst
South Ambersham
River Rother
To Selham
85ft
To Keyhurst
Midhurst to Pulborough Branch railway line

Above *Unusual design of hangar at Crail. There appears to be a similar building at Arbroath*

Below *Cranfield has now taken over as the summer venue for the Popular Flying Association Rally, held at Leicester East when DH 60G* G-ABEV *was photographed.*

Cranwell, Lincolnshire (II)

The role of Royal Air Force Cranwell is still basic flying training using Jet Provost 5As. The station stepped back in time in March 1983 when a Gloster Meteor, piloted by Squadron Leader Bruce MacDonald, swept over the airfield for the aircraft's 40th anniversary. The Jet Provost will soon be phased out now that the Ministry of Defence has selected the Shorts Tucano as the future basic trainer for the Royal Air Force. The contract will be for 130 aircraft. The first of the new trainers were due for delivery in 1986 with the balance of the Royal Air Force order spread over the following five years.

Crosby-on-Eden, Cumbria (III)

Many wartime buildings, including the Battle HQ, have now been demolished in a 'tidying-up' operation.

Crugmeer (Padstow), Cornwall

See Padstow.

Culdrose, Cornwall (V)

Apart from more building on the domestic site and the re-routing of the minor road to Gweek further south of the airfield there have been few visible changes at Culdrose in recent years. No 706 Squadron has been split in two, spawning 810 Squadron as an advanced training unit using the Sea King HAS 5, and is also updating to the more effective Mk 5 version of the aircraft. Amongst the operational units which use Culdrose as a shore base is the re-formed 849 Squadron—a most significant addition. Operating Sea King AEW 2s equipped with Searchwater radar, this unit provides the Fleet with the early-warning cover so sorely missed during the Falklands' campaign.

Dalcross, Highland (VII)

No 7 Gliding School formed here by May 1946 and was present until at least December 1952.

Dale, Dyfed (III)

No 762 Squadron moved to Halesworth on December 8 1945. The airfield closed in 1949. The tower has now been demolished but one hangar survives.

Dallachy, Grampian (VII)

Mr L.J. Clarke, who was flying here with 14 PAFU in May and June 1945, comments: 'Part of the circuit featured a total r/t blackout over about 40 degrees of arc. Real spooky. Due to a "magnetic anomaly", said some.'

In July 1985 Sir Frank Whittle returned to the Royal Air Force College—62 years after he first arrived at Cranwell in 1923. Whittle was an apprentice at Cranwell before being admitted to the college as a Flight Cadet from 1926 to 1928. Sir Frank poses in front of one of his original jet engines which is today on permanent display in Trenchard Hall, RAFC Cranwell. He is flanked by a portrait of himself in Air Commodore's uniform (his rank on retirement) and also shown is a photograph of the E28/39.

Debden, Essex (I)

The attention of readers is directed to the map on page 93 of *Action Stations 1* where some time during production the centre example of the three 225-ft 'C' Type hangars was inadvertently blotted out. It can be added within the semi-circle produced by its two flanking hangars. In the 1950s and to 1961 Debden was listed as Duxford's standby station, able to accept two short-range day fighter squadrons.

Since the RAF left in April 1975 Debden has been in Army hands as Carver Barracks.

Defford, Hereford and Worcester (III)

The first-ever automatic landing was performed here in October 1944 by Boeing 247D *DZ203*. Aircraft equipment was Rebecca and Distance Measuring Equipment with auto-homing and auto-orbiting designed by Flying Officer Barber. The ground system was an American SCS 51 localiser and glidepath. This was the original ILS and the forerunner of ILS as we know it today and was sent to Defford for demonstration to the 8th Air Force. The pilot was the late Squadron Leader J. Stewart, DFC, AFC. The 'black box' was designed by Lieutenant Colonel Francis Moseley, USAAF, who is generally credited with designing the first military ILS.

Dishforth, Yorkshire (IV)

After the departure of No 242 Operational Conversion Unit in December 1961, the Headquarters unit remained and housed Headquarters 23 Group, No 60 Maintenance Unit and a Police Provost Headquarters. Wing Commander Robert Sage, OBE, AFC, was Station Commander 1961-62. It was not until No 60 Maintenance Unit moved to Leconfield in 1965 and No 23 Group moved to Linton-on-Ouse that the station was reduced to Care and Maintenance.

In 1958 Dishforth was one of three establishments selected to conduct comparative experiments with different methods of running catering. In the case of Dishforth, the NAAFI contracted to run and staff all three messes including the bars and social arrangements. This proved successful after a diffident start and remained in force until the station closed.

With the closure of Leeming for redevelopment there have been a few changes and Linton-on-Ouse now uses Dishforth airfield.

Dover (St Margarets), Kent (IX)

During the 1920s Swingate Down was used by the Tank Corps (and doubtless other army units) for manoeuvres supported by detachments from No 2 Squadron, Manston. The squadron's 'Brisfits' flew from the old World War 1 aerodrome at St Margarets, specially reopened for the exercises, and performed impossible looking feats with suitably modified message hooks—achieving pick-ups from tanks. This hair-raising scheme apparently worked well if the tank was stationary, but was rather more difficult when it was under way!

Probably the last aeronautical use of the aerodrome was in 1966 when some of the scenes for that marvellous film *Those Magnificent Men in their Flying Machines*

Dornoch SLG seen from the cathedral tower circa 1945, with Robin hangar and numerous Lancasters and Beaufighters in open storage (via D.A. Goskirk).

were enacted at St Margarets. Some of the First World War buildings still survive though their numbers are dwindling.

Downham Market, Norfolk (I)

The improved A10 road/Downham Market bypass crosses directly across one-time Downham airfield and portions of the runway and a few buildings can still be seen. Downham had the customary three-runway layout, 093/267 of 1,900 yd and two of 1,400 yd, 034/180 and 337/157. Its two 'T2' hangars were supplemented by a Type 'B1' and three 'T2's for Horsa glider maintenance. Thirty-six frying pan dispersals were built here.

Dumfries, Dumfries and Galloway (VII)

Intended also to house an Armament Training Station as a lodger to the ASU. Mr L.J. Clarke, a staff pilot at Dumfries, comments: 'You state that 10 OAFU changed its name to 10 ANS in July 1945 and moved to Chipping Warden the following month. In fact, my log book records that the name change and the move both took place over July 10 and 11 1945.'

Dundonald, Strathclyde (VII)

Mr W.G. Wallace, an ATC cadet at that time, tells me that the landing strip at nearby Barrassie was for Spitfires being repaired at the local waggon works. The strip can still be made out, as can the wire mesh runways at Dundonald.

Dunkeswell, Devon (V)

Club and private flying continues from this airfield high up in the Blackdown Hills on the Devon/Somerset border. In September 1983 it was the venue for the British National Aerobatic Championships, but more surprisingly was the location for some semi-military activity during 1984.

As part of a development programme for new high-performance propellers a specially instrumented Gannet AEW 3 was used by Dowty-Rotol Ltd during June/July for airborne tests, the aircraft flying over measuring equipment set up on the ground at Dunkeswell. The airfield was chosen for its otherwise quiet environment, though this was doubtless broken later in the year when a reunion of the United States Navy's wartime Fleet Air Wing 7 was held in the West Country and many old comrades visited Dunkeswell.

The specially instrumented Gannet AEW 3 which was tested at Dunkeswell during the summer of 1984

Dunsfold, Surrey (IX)

The Hawker flight test facility moved from Langley to Dunsfold on September 7 1951, thus enabling the prototype Hunter *(P1067)* to leave Boscombe Down and operate from a company airfield for the first time.

Currently the AV-8B/Harrier GR 5 is the main product of the Dunsfold production line, but small batches of Sea Harriers continue to be built to special order, and development of the delightful Hawk continues.

Duxford, Cambridgeshire (I)

Adjacent to junction of M11 and A505.

Duxford is strongly established as a leading aviation museum, one of the few with an active airfield alongside giving it added attraction. Administered by the Imperial War Museum and Cambridgeshire County Council, it is daily open to view from about Easter to the end of October and mounts summer flying displays. On December 9 1985 a new hangar came into use, able to shelter large exhibits such as the Vulcan and Boeing B-29 which the Museum has acquired since 1979. The fly-

Top *'Sally B' on her arrival at Duxford as* N17TE.

Above 485784, *'Sally B', has carved a very special niche among all who delight in aged aeroplanes.*

in of the first British Concorde was for Duxford's fraternity a great event, but even more amazing was the landing of the Boeing B-52D-40-W *56-0689*, an ex-7th BW whose B-36s used to drone this way. It came not long after daybreak on October 8 1983. Impressive as they are such things seem so incongruous to anyone to whom Duxford was an RAF fighter station, and when one roams between buildings so much part of the 1920s and 1930s one still expects to come face to face with a puttied airman or a Bristol Bulldog.

Nevertheless, Duxford has undergone a considerable face lift. On non-flying summer days one can still dream very easily, when enjoying a 'garden seat' beneath the trees, of 19 Squadron's Gauntlets and Spitfires, seeing beyond an interesting line of airliners—VC-10, Britannia, Viscount, Trident 2 and Herald. There is a cafe, bookshop and an opportunity to view restoration work being undertaken on a variety of aircraft. Open hangars have something to satisfy all tastes, large guns and military vehicles included. Using a 200 ASA film and wide angle lens it is generally possible to photograph effectively most of the exhibits. Among items of particular interest are parts of the Messerschmitt Bf 110 in which Rudolf Hess flew into captivity in Scotland.

Duxford will always be the RAF home of the Spitfire and two flying examples are often here, along with Stephen Grey's exotic fighters. Further rare aircraft are often parked on the ASP. It is while viewing them that one can ponder upon what might have been, for it is now permissible to write of the post-war plans for Duxford.

On January 1 1947 the decision was made to place three short-range day figher squadrons (24 aircraft) at Duxford, the pilots being given air-to-ground firing training at Denghie Flats. The station was hardly tuned to the jet age, though, with some PSP supplementing its grass runways (NE/SW 2,000 yd, NW/SE 1,600 yd and N/S of 1,400 yd), 47 steel hardstandings and 26 hardstandings for twin-engined aircraft. The three Belfast Truss hangar units were still supplemented by eight Blister hangars. When in December 1947 Duxford's future was again reviewed the aerodrome was seen to be unsuitable for the operation of Meteor 4s with which day fighter squadrons would soon equip. These needed hard surface runways of 2,000 yd which Duxford did not possess. Consequently it was decided to move Duxford's Meteors, possibly to Martlesham or to Manston, and to earmark Duxford as a night fighter station to accommodate four Mosquito squadrons. At the same time both Coltishall and Wattisham would each have four long-range fighter (ie, intruder/escort) squadrons each of eight aircraft. Duxford was far from ideal for night fighters and so its role was virtually exchanged with that of Coltishall. In 1949 it was earmarked as a base first for Hornet long-range intruders of 19 and 41 Squadrons, soon changed to Hornets of 64 and 65 Squadrons. The intention was to supplement these with a Canberra intruder squadron and then replace the Hornets with Canberra 8s.

British defence policy vacillates daily, or so it seems, and Duxford was instead given a necessary concrete 06/24 runway of 2,000 yd, shortened to 4,931 ft when the M11 motorway arrived to ruin dear old Duxford. The runway could never have reached 9,000 ft, Duxford's buildings were really too limited to support three intruder squadrons and equally difficult was the siting of concrete dispersals for expected heavier jet fighters. The unusual shape of the site also restricted its development and made quick reaction response and scrambling very difficult although a PSP south runway was laid for use by aircraft dispersed on the airfield's south side.

Nevertheless, Duxford became one of the 19 fighter airfields ordered in summer 1950 to have a concrete runway, and later one of the limited number whose hardstandings had concrete revetment protection. The runway was completed in spring 1951 and three intruder squadrons, equipped now with 48 Hornets, were scheduled to move in when the decision to use all available Hornets in Malaya for anti-terrorist operations was agreed. Instead, the Duxford Wing would comprise only two Meteor 8 jet SRD (ie, short-range day fighter) squadrons, Nos 64 and 65 each armed with 16 and then 22 Meteors. This was soon being looked upon as a temporary feature with both squadrons earmarked for Hunters and scheduled to move to Horsham St Faith in 1955 when the two squadrons there, Nos 74 and 245, were proficient with the Swift F7 armed with Fireflash missiles. The move was thought advisable because the Hunter's duration/range was inferior to the Swift's. But the Swift was a dismal disappointment and the move became pointless. Duxford could not accommodate two day and one all-weather squadrons and so instead No 64 became an all-weather squadron because of the dire shortage of night defences. A new 'T' Hangar and technical site were added at which Meteor night fighters of 64 Squadron and later its Javelins were based. Duxford's present 'T' hangar is not that one, but another which was acquired from Tempsford.

Dyce, Grampian (VII)

Kintore was the Works Repair Depot for 15 Works Area, Air Ministry Works Directorate, for the holding of plant and stores for airfield maintenance. Fresson's original hangar is still to be seen here.

East Fortune, Lothian (VII)

No 2 Gliding School was present circa 1945.

East Haven, Tayside (VII)

The Deck Landing Training School was 769 Squadron. The station remained in use to accommodate apprentices from Arbroath, being finally closed in 1949.

Ellough (Beccles), Suffolk

See Beccles.

Errol, Tayside (VII)

No 9 Gliding School formed here by June 1945 and went to Perth late in 1946. A Hunter from 43 Squadron at Leuchars force-landed in the 1950s. In 1946 all the WAAFs were posted away and their site became 274 PoW Camp.

Eshott, Northumberland (VII)

Most of the buildings on the airfield have been cleared but derelict dispersed sites still exist. The Training Site beside the main road contains a partly demolished dummy ops room identical to the one at Rednal in Shropshire.

Evanton, Highland (VII)

Now bisected by the A9 trunk road realignment.

Firefly over Eglinton in the 1950s.

Exeter, Devon (V)

During April 1984 the operational control of the airport was transferred from Devon County Council to British Airports International, a company jointly owned by International Aeradio and the British Airports Authority. Brymon Airways, Air UK and Jersey European are the principal operators but many other companies use Exeter for summer holiday charter work and it is expected that a more aggressive marketing policy will further increase both scheduled and charter traffic.

A recent £4 million improvement programme included runway extensions, new lighting, an enlarged aircraft parking area and the introduction of surveillance radar. The impressive terminal is now complete and includes a pleasant open viewing terrace overlooking the aircraft parking stands. In much less accessible parts of the airfield an aircraft maintenance firm does steady business and at least one 'surprise' item can be seen during most visits—albeit at a distance. In addition to the terminal building terrace there is a good viewing position on the western boundary from which aircraft taxying to and from the main runway can be seen to advantage.

Fairwood Common, West Glamorgan (III)

The site was selected on June 9 1940 when the aerodrome situation after the Fall of France was critical. The choice was less than ideal and at least one Commanding Officer complained that it was dangerous, owing to 'excessive slopes and changes of gradient'.

Fearn, Highland (VII)

The original smaller tower still exists.

Felixstowe, Suffolk (I)

Still expanding and greatly flourishing is Felixstowe container port which has engulfed the one-time seaplane station. Not only that, 1984 saw the demise of one of East Anglia's most long-lived aviation features, Felixstowe's huge hangar which in two months or so was reduced to a pile of scrap metal. The pre-war watch office and tower remain on what used to seem a very extensive concrete apron, along with just one hangar. Very little remains of Britain's maritime aviation, so it was certainly sad to see that large hangar dying. But its end might have come sooner for within the upper part was discovered a bomb, probably placed there in 1942.

Early editions of Volume 1 refer to the Bv 13—meaning Bv 138, and the MAEE disbanded on July 31 1958 and not in 1950. A reader, Ian Gillies, recalled that in 1951 the MAEE staff were looking forward to working on the Saro Princess and thought it likely that official trials would be conducted at Cowes instead of Felixstowe. Between 1949 and 1951 MAEE Felixstowe handled the Short Sealand,

Supermarine Seagull, SR/A1 jet, Sunderlands, Seafords and Solents. Survival equipment, airborne lifeboats and dinghies were also tested. Also there at this time was 1103 MCU whose boats tended the seaplanes and operated an ASR service. In terms of personnel the station's most important function was as the domestic site for the now long defunct Trimley radar, a GCI station for Metropolitan Sector of Fighter Command.

Feltwell, Norfolk (I)

Although technically still an RAF station, Feltwell has a most novel role for the buildings around its barrack square now house classrooms, study centres, a library and a mixture of other educational items that together form the home for the American Lakenheath Middle School. One hangar serves as a sumptuous indoor sports hall, but others are used by the Americans as storage centres. In wartime, part of Feltwell would become a hospital. Very few airfields, and none as elaborate as the permanent peacetime RAF Feltwell, have become schools. What splendid history lessons one could produce at Feltwell! Incidentally, there were never any hard surface runways here, only three marked grass runways. There were, however, 20 circular hardstandings.

Filton, Avon (V)

The reference to Luftwaffe attacks on Filton in *Action Stations 5* needs some qualification. Erprobungsgruppe 210 did not lead in KG55 on September 25 (they

Below *It can snow at Exeter too! An evocative shot of a 263 Squadron twin-engined Whirlwind fighter dispersed at the airport in January 1941* (via J. Munro).

Bottom *Looking north across Exeter from the airport buildings during 1944. The petrol pumps, or their modern equivalents, are still in the same position but the RAF bowsers, Chance Light and the Blister hangars have long since disappeared—as has the overflying Spitfire!* (via H. Holmes).

were attacking Portland) and the Luftwaffe's target on the 27th was Yate, though this was not apparent at the time.

The Americans made considerable use of Filton as Station 803, three units of the Tactical Air Command of the 9th Air Force arriving between November 28 and December 3 1943 to re-assemble P-38, P-47, P-51, A-20, AT-6, C-64 and C-78 aircraft which had been shipped across the Atlantic into Avonmouth docks. USAAF personnel at Filton numbered some 500 and facilities included four Butler Combat hangars, which were transportable sheds resembling enlarged 'Robin' types. During their six-month stay numerous aircraft were assembled and flight-tested before despatch to the rapidly increasing number of operational 9th AF units in southern England. Serious accidents were few, but a test pilot was killed in a crash near Filton on February 9 1944 and 16 men were injured the following June when one of the Butler hangars collapsed while being dismantled prior to departure of the USAAF units—their work complete following the landings in Normandy.

The Rolls-Royce test fleet is still present at Filton though sadly depleted, while BAe's main activity is centred on the refurbishing and modernisation of USAF F-111s and work on Airbus wings.

Finningley, Yorkshire (IV)

In 1983 the basic Air Loadmaster training returned to Finningley as an integral part of the Air Electronics and Air Engineering school. The Air Loadmaster Training Squadron commenced training on April 18 with an intake of five students. The school's building has been completely refurbished to fit its new role and now has a large indoor working area with a dummy aircraft floor for developing loading and restraint techniques; a stressed roof beam with a power winch for simulating helicopter underslung loads; and various items of aircraft restraint equipment.

During 1984 and 1985 there were many rumours that mining subsidence would force the closure of Royal Air Force Finningley, but it is probable that Finningley will continue as an RAF station for the forseeable future.

Ford, West Sussex (IX)

A combined detachment made up of crews from the 422nd and 425th Night Fighter Squadrons, USAAF, flew their P-61 Black Widows into Ford on July 15 1944 to join the hard-pressed defenders of London in defeating the V-1 (flying bomb) menace. The very next night Lieutenant Ernst spotted the tell-tale exhausts of four V-1s approaching the south coast. They were easy to see but difficult to attack at night and his first pass had to be broken off. He then dived on a second and with two short bursts of fire hit the pulse jet engine and the V-1 went straight into the Channel off Beachy Head.

After about a fortnight's operations the P-61s were withdrawn from Ford, but during that brief period two Black

Jetstreams from the Multi-Engine Training Squadron being refuelled at Finningley.

Sea King ZA105 *outside a hangar at Finningley in September 1983. This helicopter was used by the Prime Minister's team while in the Falklands. It was turned from yellow to grey overnight for the visit, the work being carried out at Finningley. The Prime Minister herself flew in* XZ592.

Widows had been damaged by exploding 'doodlebugs'—they were very nasty things to tackle!

Fordoun, Grampian (VII)

The suggested ATC Gliding School was in fact formed here by October 1944 as No 5 GS and moved to Dyce in May 1946.

Framlingham, Suffolk (I)

Framlingham is well worth a visit for the wartime control tower illustrated in *Action Stations 1* has become a museum devoted to the airfield's history. Best to check to ensure that it is going to be open before making a call. Light aircraft operate from the airfield which is now known as Parham. During the war it had three concrete and tar runways whose surfaces were topped with wood chips. There were two 'T2' hangars here and 50 loop dispersals.

Gatwick, West Sussex (VIII)

Gatwick maintained its growth in passenger traffic with an overall increase of 11.6 per cent to 14.2 million in 1984/85. With growth in air transport movements of only 3.7 per cent, the average number of passengers per flight increased to 108.

Aerial view of Foulsham in August 1978. Its relatively healthy state resulted from its being long earmarked for post-war use.

Despite improvements to the South Terminal, the airport's passenger facilities now face increasing pressure until the North Terminal enters service in 1987. Projects completed during 1985 include a significant increase in size of the duty-free facilities and the opening of a second parallel taxiway.

Gosport, Hants (IX)

On the demise of HMS *Siskin* in June 1956 Gosport was recommissioned as HMS *Sultan*, the Royal Naval School of Marine Engineering. This unit has used the hangars as workshops and other buildings as classrooms for the past 30 years and following recent re-organisation of naval training the school is being further expanded and will take in more of the old airfield. It is now the largest Royal Navy ground training establishment in the country.

Grangemouth, Central (VII)

The county in which the airfield is situated is Central, not Strathclyde. KLM DC-3 *PH-ASR* visited on the day it opened, flying in guests from Holland. No 2 Gliding School re-formed here on November 1 1947 and was present until at least September 1949. No 6 GS had formed here by May 1945 but went to Turnhouse about a year later.

Graveley, Cambridgeshire (I)

The last RAF aircraft to take off from this airfield did so on July 16 1964. Graveley had been used as an RLG by Oakington which subsequently made limited use of Waterbeach.

Great Saling (Andrewsfield), Essex

See Andrewsfield.

Great Sampford, Essex (I)

It is now known that this primitive airfield was in 1944 and into 1945 administered by Balloon Command. In 1944, during the time that the Regiment Battle School was here, Great Sampford was used for practice landings by heavy gliders. Sampford in 1943-45 had two Sommerfeld Tracking runways, 23/05 of 1,600 yd and 307/127 of 1,050 yd. Four Over Type Blister hangars, six hardstandings for small fighters and nine concrete dispersals were available, along with accommodation for 34 officers, 106 SNCOs and 669 other ranks. To make it more homely housing was also provided for five SNCO WAAFs and 60 other ranks.

Greencastle, Down (VII)

The 5th CCRC was established here in November 1943 for B-24 crews, but transferred, on paper, to Cheddington on February 20 1944. Personnel then joined other units at Greencastle and Mullaghmore.

Grove, Oxfordshire (VI)

Many airfields are from time to time occupied by 'ground' units, small in strength and very difficult to keep record of. One such was No 431 Equipment Depot, 2nd TAF, with which Danny Nelson of Margate served. He recalls that he arrived at 431 ED, Grove on July 14 1954, shortly after the airfield had been re-opened for the first time since closure in 1946. He left just before it closed again, about September 1955. Grove's task had been to supply 2 TAF with many of its needs, but not as originally planned. Runways had been resurfaced and flying control reactivated before it was realised that heavy transport operations could not be supported. Instead, such supplies as arrived had to be flown to Germany, mainly from Lyneham. Training flights were carried out from Grove.

Guernsey, Channel Isles (V)

In July 1917 a French seaplane base was built on the southern side of St Peter Port harbour, accommodation huts being erected by the Royal Navy and a Bessoneaux hangar sent from France. The base was established for 12 seaplanes but the build-up was slow, only two being on strength by the end of July. Despite this the establishment was raised to 16 patrol planes in September and by the end of the year 11 Tellier and ten FBA flying boats were on strength.

The chosen site proved difficult operationally, the only practical take-off and landing runs becoming very tricky in the frequent strong winds experienced during the winter. The canvas roof of the hangar also suffered frequent storm damage and the Commandant, Lieutenant de Vaisseau le Cour Grandmaison, recommended transfer of the base to Cherbourg. Despite reduced activity following damage to the seaplane crane early in 1918 his advice was ignored and the unit remained in Guernsey until December 1918. The aircraft were then flown to Cherbourg and the detachment of 150 men soon followed.

According to records held in the Channel Islands the bombing attack on St Peter Port on June 28 1940 was carried out by He 111s of KG27, not Ju 87 dive-bombers as usually stated.

Halton, Buckinghamshire (VI)

Mr D.C. King has long lived close to Halton and points out that more should have been included about Halton's flying activities. A very active aerodrome pre-war, the landing ground had to be extended by about a third in 1935 to cope with modern, fast aircraft and that cost a local farmer, Mr Tenby, two of his fields. No night flying took place at that time and because of the lie of the land flying had to take place on the NE/SW axis. A permanent flying control tower was built circa 1940, and a Gliding School for 1365 ATC Squadron opened in 1942. Halton also knew something of the operational side of events with on one occasion a 'shot-up' B-17 slithering to a halt across the Halton-Weston Turville road. With Chequers close by there was VIP traffic too, one load of visitors dying when in 1944 their Dakota crashed into the Chilterns during its approach.

Hardwick Park, Derbyshire (III)

Note that the correct MAP title for this SLG is Hardwick Park. Rendel, Palmer and Tritton were the consultant engineers for the SLGs, rather than contractors.

Harwell, Oxfordshire (VI)

Harwell suffered badly from typesetting errors in Volume 6, wrote Eric Cannings who also pointed out that he and Ryman devised the 'Harwell Boxes'. These, not the towers mentioned, were copied by other units and were Celestial Navigation Trainers. Also on page 158... Harwell had a bomb dump, NOT a boat dump! Eric Cannings was the first of many readers to enjoy the reference on page 65 to the Metrovack F/2 engine. A sort of big boy's vacuum cleaner? Nay, just a misprint of Metrovick F/2. Other print errors noticed were on page 210, Lysse which should be Liss, and on page 211 Berrisfield which should be Berinsfield.

Hatfield, Hertfordshire (VIII)

In June 1983 the Royal Air Force took delivery of its first BAe 146 for military routes in Europe. It was handed over to Air Marshal Sir Peter Bairsto, Deputy Commander-in-Chief Strike Command, by Air Chief Marshal Sir Dennis Smallwood, Military Adviser to British Aerospace. The ceremony took place at Hatfield on June 14 and in the log book for the new medium-range transport aircraft it was designated BAe 146 C Mark 1 by the Royal Air Force.

This was the first of two aircraft and, after the hand-over ceremony, the '146 was flown from Hatfield to Brize Norton via Northolt by Squadron Leader David Gale with Flight Lieutenant Michael Jones as co-pilot. The normal aircrew for the 146 is four—pilot, co-pilot and two cabin staff. At Brize Norton the aircraft was attached to No 241 Operational Conversion Unit as 146 Evaluation Flight. The aircraft was soon put into intensive use, being ideal for short haul routes from Brize Norton to West Germany. In 1985

British Aerospace BAe 146 on its first flight in September 1981.

Top *Non-standard pillbox built into the side of a culvert at Hawarden, with the water tower in the background.*

Above *Mustang 1 painted on the wall of 41 OTU's Flight Office at Hawarden. Seen in 1984.*

the two evaluation aircraft were returned to BAe Hatfield, and the Royal Air Force ordered two '146s for the Queen's Flight.

Haverfordwest, Dyfed (III)

Plans to move 6 (O) AFU here from Staverton were abandoned in February 1944. No 4 RFU disbanded on January 4 1945. There was an ELG known as Haroldston five miles west of Haverfordwest.

Hawarden, Clwyd (III)

The 'Broughton Wellington', *R1333*, survived the air raid on November 14 1940 only to be destroyed in a take-off crash at Newmarket a few weeks later. As a propaganda and morale-boosting exercise in 1944 a Wellington was assembled in the factory in 24 hours 48 minutes, a film being made of the event. No 173 Squadron formed out of 4 (Home) Ferry Unit on February 1 1953. In May 1985 the British Aerospace factory celebrated the sale of its 600th BAe 125 business jet.

Heathfield (Ayr), Strathclyde *see Ayr*

Heathrow, London (VIII)

In 1986 the new Terminal 4 opened at Heathrow, providing the airport with the capacity to handle an additional 2,000 passengers per hour in each direction. Constructed away from the central area on the south side of the airport, with its own London Underground link, it is the first terminal at Heathrow to segregate incoming and outgoing passengers completely on two separate floor levels. There are 22 new aircraft gates and 64 check-in desks to minimise queuing.

Heathrow has been at the hub of world

civil aviation for more than 30 years and, as Mike King, airport Director, says, 'A fully integrated four-terminal system guarantees that place for the future'.

Helensburgh, Strathclyde (VII)

The large assembly hangar still exists. Sunderland Road and Blackburn Road recall the aviation associations, the original houses in these roads being aluminium prefabs made in the factory just after the war. Among the many marine aircraft brought here for trials were the floatplane Spitfire, the Saro 37 with scaled-down Shetland floats fitted, and examples of the Skua and Roc with floats. The Roc was found to be dangerously unstable and it crashed on take-off on December 3 1939. With some modifications a second aircraft was tested, including some fresh water take-offs from Loch Lomond, but it was not a success.

Below *Night scene at London Heathrow—Boeing 747B of Swissair being loaded.*

Bottom *Heathrow's new Terminal 4 with its mile-long perimeter while under construction.*

Aerial view of RAF Hemswell technical and domestic site which was sold in 1985.

Hell's Mouth, Gwynedd (III)

Recategorised as an ELG on May 1 1944.

Hemswell, Lincolnshire (II)

By 1985 the runways had gone and the airfield had been sold to First State Holdings who have purchased many wartime airfields, including Faldingworth, Middleton St George, Colerne, and Halton. The airfield was split into lots and sold in October 1985. A variety of offices and businesses have turned the old Technical Site into a useful complex, retaining in the process the wartime buildings.

In September 1985 plans were well underway by a businessman to retain the Headquarters Building in its wartime state and turn it into the 'Headquarters' Public House. It will have a restaurant with a special reunion room and bars with steward service to the lounges. Some of the main wartime rooms will house wartime documents and photographs and be open to the public at certain times. The Headquarters Building is a rare three-storey building and deserves to be preserved.

Henstridge, Dorset (V)

The uncertain situation at Henstridge was finally resolved at the end of 1986. The BBC who had purchased part of the 350-acre airfield in 1979, and British Telecom who later submitted plans for a satellite communications receiving station on the site, prevented flying over their land and at one stage the owner of Aly Aviation only had access to the hangar and the surrounding apron, and only helicopters could operate from the site. After years of argument and appeals both the BBC and British Telecom were refused planning permission and in 1986 a local businessman acquired most of the airfield which re-opened for fixed-wing flying in November 1986. It had been a long fight but local persistence had paid off and for once an airfield was saved —for the immediate future at least.

High Ercall, Shropshire (III)

No 60 OTU formed here on May 17 1943. Among the aircraft on 29 MU's scrap dump logged by the Rev John Durnell on January 12 1946 were Bermuda I *FF532, FF534,* several Turbinlite Havocs, Ventura *FN959/G* with USAAF and RAF markings, Lodestar *G-AGDC* and an all-silver Spitfire IX *EN775* with code *C* in black.

High Wycombe, Buckinghamshire (VIII)

On November 18 1983, No 1 Group and No 38 Group amalgamated to form an enlarged No 1 Group with its headquarters at Upavon. Royal Air Force Strike Command, with its headquarters at High Wycombe, has overall control of all front-line aircraft of the Royal Air Force within the United Kingdom and worldwide with the exception of those in Royal Air Force Germany. These aircraft, their bases and personnel, will now be administered and operated by three Groups—No 1, No 11 and No 18.

No 1 Group has moved from Bawtry in Yorkshire to the former No 38 Group headquarters at Upavon in order to maintain the strong links between the Royal Air Force and the Army. No 1 is now the largest Group within Strike Command. Its aircraft include the new strike/attack Tornados; offensive support Jaguars and Harriers; air-to-air refuelling TriStars, VC-10s, Victors and Hercules; battlefield support Puma and Chinook helicopters and air transport VC-10s and Hercules.

No 11 Group will continue to be responsible for air defence. Its assets include Phantom and Lightning interceptors (and in the near future the air defence variant of the Tornado), Hawk day fighters and air defence radars and surface-to-air missiles. It is also being equipped with an airborne early warning version of the Nimrod. Its headquarters remain at Bentley Priory in North London.

No 18 Group is co-located with the Royal Navy's Fleet headquarters in Northwood, Middlesex, and is involved with maritime operations. It controls Nimrod anti-submarine and maritime patrol aircraft, Buccaneer anti-shipping strike/attack aircraft and search and rescue helicopters.

The reorganisation follows the demise of the Vulcan bomber, formerly operated by No 1 Group, and its replacement by the much smaller Tornado multi-role combat aircraft; thereby enabling a streamlining of the organisation of Strike Command and consequent cost savings.

Hinstock (Ollerton), Shropshire (III)

The original SLG buildings can still be seen just to the north of the aerodrome.

Hixon, Staffordshire (III)

The tower has now been renovated for offices and a painting from the well-known Imperial War Museum photo hangs in the former control room.

Holme-on-Spalding Moor, Yorkshire (IV)

As Buccaneer *XV350* took to the air on Wednesday, December 7 1983, it brought to an end the last Buccaneer movement from Holme-on-Spalding Moor. It was piloted by chief test pilot Roger Searle and in the back seat was Mike Edwards, General Manager of British Aerospace. On Thursday December 15 British Aerospace's days at the airfield came to an end. Most of the workload from Holme-on-Spalding Moor moved to Brough, the remainder to Royal Air Force Scampton where British Aerospace have leased some land and erected two mini-hangars (qv). The airfield at Holme-on-Spalding Moor has been bought by the Fisher Thompson Group based at Hutton Cranswick, near Driffield.

Honington, Suffolk (I)

Honington in the 1970s was the home of the Buccaneer, and remained so until the summer of 1983. But change crept in earlier with the opening of the Tornado Weapons Conversion Unit which received its first Tornado GR 1 in June 1981 and began training crews at the end of that year. Late in 1983 its aircraft started to display the markings of No 45 Squadron, emphasising the unit's role as a training one with operational capability.

Major building work on Honington's north side resulted in the erection of HASs to shelter the Tornados which increased in number when, on June 1 1982, No IX Squadron re-formed here with GR 1s and became the first RAF squadron to use the Hardened Aircraft Shelters. These are backed by operations and maintenance sections in further hardened and NBC proofed buildings. They also feature something else unusual, an all-ranks restaurant. Arrival of so many Tornados could mean only one thing, that all the Buccaneers would need to move. No 12 Squadron vacated Honington in October 1982 and joined 8 Squadron, its one time companion, at

Lossiemouth, to where 237 OCU moved in October 1984. No 208 Squadron's Buccaneers left Honington in July 1983 and 216 Squadron, which formed here on December 2 1978 and moved to Lossiemouth in July 1980. IX Squadron and the TWCU currently occupy the all-Tornado station.

Honington has long been an important operational RAF station, yet it was not until after the war that it was provided with permanent hard runways, wartime Honington making do with a 2,000 yd 10/28 steel mat runway supported by grass NE/SW and SE/NW runways of 1,400 yd. Its four 'C' Type hangars remain, but not the nine Blisters, and the 75 wartime hardstandings have long since been overtaken.

Hooton Park, Cheshire (III)

No 5 FTS used the aerodrome in 1934 and presumably some time afterwards for forced-landing practice at a rent of £50 per annum. About 330 yd of runway and the large apron which was designed to park two squadrons of Meteors remain in good condition. Firing butts and a gymnasium are among the surviving buildings. Some small parts from scrapped Mosquitoes, identifiable by stamped numbers, were found in 1984.

Horsham St Faith, Norfolk (I)

Horsham now flourishes as Norwich Airport, but its military past is recalled in a growing museum on the airfield's north side where resides an incongruous Vulcan near the site chosen for a new terminal complex. For many years, Hethel had a connection with Horsham, being its post-war standby airfield.

In recent years Norwich has been a happy hunting ground for Fokker F 27 Friendship spotters. AirUK operates them through Norwich to which airfield other F 27s have been coming for facelifts and the acquisition of a very appealing 'wide bodied look'. Norwich also receives numerous businessmen's flights, Short SD 360s, Cessnas, Pipers, etc. Apart from the Goodyear Europa Airship here in 1982, undoubtedly the most amazing sight of the early 1980s was the ultimate in 'wide bodies', the RAF's first TriStar which, on a bright Saturday afternoon in September 1985, astonished the whole of Norwich by its presence during a mighty 'roller' along the 6,043-ft asphalt and concrete LCGIV 09/27 runway.

Humberside (Kirmington), Lincolnshire

See Kirmington.

Hurn, Dorset (V)

Various light plane organisations flourish and Flight Refuellings' interests at Hurn have multiplied rapidly over the past few years, but this welcome increase in activity has been more than offset by the closure of the BAe factory. The erstwhile production sheds now hold EEC 'intervention' grain while other parts of the factory have been used for aircraft storage. Negotiations over the development of the airport buildings, a hotel, houses, shopping centre and leisure complex have been progressing for over six years.

Inskip, Lancashire (III)

Other planned FAA stations in the north-west which would have had strong connections with Inskip, had they been built, were Midge Hall near Preston (fighter practice station), Cuddington in Cheshire (fighter training), Abergele in Clwyd (TBR training) and Guilden Sutton near

HB-*serialled Argus III at Hooton Park in July 1944. This aircraft was used for taxi and communications work by Martin Hearn Ltd (No 7 Aircraft Assembly Unit)* (via M. Hearn).

The tower at Jurby in 1945. The airmen are sweeping up glass shattered when a crash-landed Sunderland blew up on the runway.

Chester (disembarkation station for carriers using Liverpool). Sites at Myn-Rhos and Rhyl in North Wales are also quoted but they may be alternative names for Abergele. Construction of all of them was refused, mainly because of the serious loss of fertile agricultural land and the fact that the end of the war was in sight.

Jersey, Channel Islands (V)

The Admiralty took over Jersey Airport at the beginning of March 1940 when 755 Squadron moved in from Worthy Down. Their Shark biplanes then flew navigational exercises in the comparative seclusion of the Western Approaches to the English Channel. They were joined for a week's flying training by Albacores of 826 (not 828) Squadron in May but had been hastily evacuated to Lee-on-Solent by the end of the month because of the German breakthrough in France.

It now appears from records held in the Channel Islands that the bombing of the La Rocque and Weighbridge harbour areas of St Helier on June 28 1940 was executed by six He 111s of KG27, not the legendary Stukas so often blamed in the past.

Kemble, Gloucestershire (V)

The Red Arrows have gone to Scampton but Kemble has been reprieved and with little more than a temporary pause is now operating as the Support Center Europe of the USAF Logistics Command (AFLC/SCE), following a unique agreement between the British and American governments. Largely staffed by British civilians and commanded by a RAF Wing Commander, the base also accommodates a number of American Service and civilian personnel to provide expertise and quality control.

Initially dealing with refurbishing of Fairchild A-10As from the 81st TFW, Bentwaters, work has also been carried out on F-4 Phantoms, OV-10s and EC-135 aircraft, in addition to overhauls of American vehicles, refuellers, fire tenders, snow ploughs and fork lift trucks. Arrester gear was installed on the runway during 1983 so that the Phantoms could be accommodated and in October of that year it was announced that a runway extension of 4,000 ft had been approved.

Seven of the 17 hangars are currently in use, one exclusively for a small RAF Support Command task—the overhaul and modification of Jetstreams, Sea Herons and Sea Devons on behalf of the Royal Navy. In 1984 it was stated that Kemble was to be the first of three forward storage sites. Based in the hangars formerly occupied by the Red Arrows, this unit will supply spares to USAF bases throughout Europe using newly purchased Short C-23A Sherpa cargo transports for the operation. Kemble's future again looks assured—while American forces remain in Europe.

Keyshill, Ayrshire

67/453230

Intended as an SLG for Prestwick to disperse the large number of aircraft awaiting onward ferrying after Transatlantic delivery. Under construction in 1941 but abandoned.

Top *An old wartime hut nestles amongst the undergrowth at Kirmington.*

Above *Humberside Airport in 1985, a hive of activity.*

Kidlington, Oxfordshire (VI)

SP472155.

Squadron Leader Geoff Phillips, MBE, points out that the Dome Trainer here was used for gunnery training in 20 (P)AFU days. During my own Service days that at Wellesbourne was certainly referred to as the Celestial Trainer, and a supply of slides in the dome depicted star groups. Did these domes have mixed uses? Wyton still has a good example, but few remain complete.

Geoff also reminds us that in 1939 Tipsy Trainers *(G-AFRV* and *G-AFVN)* were used by Airtraining (Oxford) within the Civil Air Guard scheme. For half a crown you could have taken a flying lesson. Cor! On a sadder note, though, two Oxfords were shot down by an intruder on August 12/13 1941, *R6156* and *W6629* both being flown solo.

Oxford University Air Squadron, incidentally, which used Shellingford during the war, is now known to have moved to Abingdon in 1946 and vacated that station in April 1949.

Kingstown, Cumbria (III)

The PoW escape attempt took place in November 1941. No 189 Gliding School formed here in 1945 but operations suspended October 1947.

Kirkistown, Down (VII)

Tentatively allocated to USAAF Air Support Command on February 28 1942. Allocated to the 8th Air Force as fighter base on June 4 1942. Allocation rescinded April 1943. Allocated as tactical fighter base July 12 1943 but never occupied by USAAF. Nos 808 and 885 Squadrons had already re-equipped with Hellcats before moving here from Ballyhalbert. Construction contractors were Messrs B. Sunley & Co but owing to a labour shortage some of the work was done by Army personnel.

Kirkton, Highland (VII)

Used early in the war by TT aircraft.

Local boys apparently used to be paid ten shillings (50p), a handsome sum in those days, for finding and returning lost target drogues!

Kirkwall, Orkney (VII)

Still the main air link for Orkney with mainland Scotland and the rest of the UK, it is also the axis for the inter-island air service. Three of the wartime fighter pens can still be seen here.

Kirmington (Humberside), Lincolnshire (II)

A few changes have taken place and both Eastern Airways and Lease Air have gone. Eastern was bought out and merged with two other smaller carriers to emerge as Genair, which based its operations on Humberside and established a number of successful feeder routes to other parts of Britain and to Denmark. However, Genair ran into difficulties and ceased operations in the summer of 1984. Air UK is now the main company to operate out of Humberside Airport with Short 360s and Fokker Friendships. British Airways Helicopters also use the airport, operating a shuttle service to the gas rigs in the Rough Field area of the North Sea. They have two machines permanently based at Humberside with their own support staff. In addition, Management Aviation, who are based at Strubby, regularly use Humberside Airport as part of their support for BP's West Sole field. In 1984 Humberside Executive Aviation set up its base of operation at the airport.

Air cargo is another important aspect of day-to-day operations and the air freight companies using the airport are Anglia Air Freight, Spur Air and Regional Freight Service. The airport has a customs transit shed to handle goods brought by both road and air through the airport. Humberside Airport can handle most types of aircraft engaged on freight traffic, including Boeing 737s, C-130s, DC-6s and Argosies.

Unlike some other airports, Humberside has plenty of room for growth and there are currently between 20 and 30 acres of undeveloped land within the area designated for industrial purposes. Plans are in the pipeline for the taxiway to be extended to make more development plots available for future demand.

Ambitious plans have been drawn up by the airport's owners, Humberside County Council, which would make the airport very attractive to holiday charter companies, and could bring in a wider range of short-haul scheduled services enabling Humberside to handle anything up to 400,000 passengers a year. In jargon the old wartime bomber base would understand—'Maximum Effort'.

Humberside Airport has a very bright potential future for it is close to the new £180-million road network built in Humberside in recent years. It was an ideal site for a bomber airfield and it is perfect for peacetime. It is close to the £92-million Humber Bridge and the county's road network—M62, M180, A15 and A180—puts many cities all within easy driving distance of an airport which poses no access or parking problems to motorists.

Plans are already drawn up to extend the airport's runway from 1,670 to over 2,000 yd which would open the way for much heavier aircraft on routes to the Mediterranean in the late 1980s. Both Britannia and Orion Airways have already used Humberside for proving flights for their Boeing 737s and once the runway extensions are complete and load penalties on larger aircraft removed, they will find Humberside an attractive proposition.

Knowsley Park, Merseyside (III)

During 1944 a P-61 Black Widow crashed here whilst 'beating-up' the site.

Laira, Devon

SX510554. 1½ miles E of Plymouth city centre off A38

Early in 1918 it was decided to experiment with mooring-out stations for the main RNAS operational airship bases. The primary object was to extend the patrol area covered by the 'ships', but also to reduce the risk of bad weather closing in and leaving no secure moorings within range on return from patrol.

The SSZ15 *non-rigid moored out in a wood —believed to be at Laira sub-station in 1918* (FAA Museum).

Trials were carried out by personnel from RNAS Mullion, a site on the banks of the River Plym being chosen. It was in Saltram Park, close to the old Plymouth racecourse on Chelston Meadow, conveniently screened by trees from all but an easterly wind. For the trials these same trees were used to secure a SS-type airship, and despite the *SST2* being badly damaged during a visit from Mullion on March 15 1918, the plan was declared a success. It was decided to establish a chain of mooring-out sites between the permanent stations and naturally one of them was in Saltram Park, this sub-station taking its name from the Laira district of Plymouth. With moorings for two SS or Coastal 'ships', it was commissioned in May 1918. No buildings were erected, the ratings living in the racecourse grandstand and reputedly bunking on the slatted wooden seats!

Operations under the control of the C-in-C Devonport were concentrated on anti-submarine protection for the approaches to the dockyard and for convoys passing along the south Devon coast. With the formation of No 9 Group, the RAF took command of Mullion and its sub-stations, but operational control was retained by the Naval authorities at Devonport. Patrols were largely uneventful and few problems were experienced until just before the Armistice—the *SSZ14* being wrecked at Laira on November 6.

The airships continued to fly fitfully for a month or two after the end of the war, but with the decision to abandon the use of non-rigids for sea patrol the sub-station was closed.

The old racecourse, which had been used briefly in 1911 by the well-known lady aviator, Mrs Blondeau Hewlett, was again pressed into use for barnstorming by the Berkshire Aviation Company making the most of the post-war craze for 5/- (25p) 'flips' using the ubiquitous Avro 504K. An attempt to start an air service to Croydon was made in 1923. Flown by Surrey Flying Services on behalf of the Plymouth Chamber of Commerce and local newspapers, a route-proving flight early in April was followed by another to Manchester. Naturally much publicity surrounded these events and the Civil Aviation Branch of the Air Ministry took an interest. They frowned upon the many ditches across Chelston Meadow, however, and further experimental services were flown from the polo ground at Roborough.

The joy-riding boom was soon over and the racecourse landing ground had fallen into disuse even before Roborough became the permanent home of the Plymouth & District Aero Club.

The view south-east across the main domestic site of Lake Down with the hangars and aerodrome in the background, September 1918. Amongst the trees on the opposite side of the road to the hangars is Druids Lodge, the 33rd Wing HQ (P. Liddle via G.S. Leslie).

Lake Down, Wilts

SU010393. 7 miles NNW of Salisbury alongside A360.

Early in 1917 some 160 acres of rolling pastureland close by a large house called Druids Lodge were requisitioned by the War Office for use as another Salisbury Plain flying training station. Surrounded by tumuli and barrows, it was actually built on a prehistoric field system, and maintained this connection with antiquity by being named Lake Down.

The roughly triangular landing ground was flanked on the western side by a large technical site, the construction of six paired GS sheds, a similarly sized Aeroplane Repair Shed and two MT sheds being started during the autumn. The domestic accommodation was built 1,500 ft to the north on the opposite side of the main road near Horse Down. Lake Down was connected to other military establishments on the Plain by a rail network, one spur of which terminated at what is now Druids Lodge Farm.

No 2 TDS formed at Lake Down on August 15 1917 with BE 2C, RE 8 and DH 4 aircraft but moved 'just up the road' to Stonehenge in December. It was replaced during February 1918 by No 108 Squadron, a day bomber unit which had been working-up in the shadow of the famous standing stones, and Lake Down's strength increased rapidly with the formation of No 136 Squadron on the same day as the RAF was born, and by No 107 Squadron on May 15. Before the three day-bomber squadrons could properly settle in, however, it was decided that No 14 TDS would form at Lake Down on June 6. To make room, No 107 Squadron went to France with DH 9s and all the most experienced pilots, No 108 went to Kenley, and early in July 1918 No 136 Squadron was disbanded.

Operating under the eye of No 33 Wing, which used Druids Lodge as its headquarters, No 14 TDS continued the day bomber theme by being established with 36 Avro 504K and 36 DH4/9 aircraft and a personnel strength of 858. The construction programme was virtually complete by the beginning of August 1918 and for the last three months of the 1914-18 War a full training schedule was maintained. With the Armistice came a rapid run-down in training requirements and No 14 TDS was an early casualty. It is believed to have moved to Boscombe Down by the end of the year but if so it was only in cadre form.

No 201 Squadron moved in during February 1919 to await demobilisation of personnel and disbandment, but went to Eastleigh in October when the decision to close Lake Down was taken. The bulk of the buildings on both the technical and domestic sites were gradually dismantled

Druids Lodge, the HQ of the 33rd Wing, alongside the present A360 road with Lake Down aerodrome buildings to the east. The strangely-named house has changed little over the past 68 years (P. Liddle via G.S. Leslie).

following auction, and woodland now covers most of the workshop area except for that occupied by a small number of sheds close to the road. These are probably the only remaining evidence of this well-appointed First World War aerodrome except for the large elevated water tower which was used to replenish the steam locomotives operating on the military railway.

During July 1943 the AOP Austers of No 653 Squadron spent a short time in a field close to Druids Lodge—the house, which can be glimpsed from the road through trees, still looking much the same as when it was the Wing HQ.

Lakenheath, Suffolk (I)

TL743821.

One is apt to regard Lakenheath's F-111Fs as becoming quite aged although they had only been in use for two years when *Action Stations 1* appeared in 1979. F-111s have, like the A-10s, become very much part of East Anglia of the 1980s for Upper Heyford's F-111Es also make much use of eastern air space. The major change seen at Lakenheath in the 1980s has been the extensive arrray of Hardened Aircraft Shelters in which the F-111s are mostly housed, so that on passing the base one may sometimes see none of its aircraft except a few aged machines serving as decoys. Four squadrons of F-111Fs reside here, each generally applying its authorised colour to the top of the fins of its aircraft, blue identifying the 492nd, yellow the 493rd, red the 494th and green the 495th. Aircraft drawn from the whole Wing for detachments often carry three or four colours.

Charles Bassett reminded me that in 1940-41, where the present US Air Force Gun Club is sited, several wooden dummy Wellingtons were erected as decoys forming a tempting but useless target for the enemy. Ron Clarke provided another new item, in the form of photographs of an LZVII (?) Kite Balloon (ie, barrage balloon) being tested at Lakenheath circa 1937 during trials to assess its rough weather handling, for which reason it was placed in a pit.

Lakenheath, incidentally, was expanded mainly during 1945 to accommodate bombers in the 80,000 lb+ all-up weight class, Runway 246 being extended to 3,000 yd and the other two (100 and 322) to 2,000 yd, all being concrete runways. There still remained only two 'T2' hangars and a 'B1', along with 36 hardstandings.

Langford Lodge, Antrim (VII)

The reason why Langford increasingly devoted its efforts to modification and to engineering and research was because of its inaccessibility from the combat bases in eastern England. This minimised its value as a repair depot for only 'fly-in' aircraft could economically be brought here for overhaul.

Langham, Norfolk (I)

As well as being used for anti-aircraft co-operation duties, post-war Langham was brought up to Airfield (War) Standard in the 1950s—hence the long runway. It was earmarked for two SRD fighter squadrons, with Little Snoring as its standby airfield. If you visit Langham you might see the Puss Moth now residing here. A visit to nearby North Creake is worthwhile too, for the control tower is a dwelling—complete with chimney. Quite a lot of the camp remains, for it was long in line for use post-war as a heavy bomber base.

Larkhill, Wiltshire (V)

It is now known that 'D' Flight, the first AOP unit, moved to Larkhill on June 2 1940 fresh from its abruptly terminated 'field' trials in France.

Some of the original aeroplane sheds erected before World War 1 still exist at the southern end of Wood Road, Larkhill Army Camp. They are in use as barrack stores.

Leconfield, Yorkshire (IV)

During the period 1945 to 1957 Leconfield became associated with the Empire Air Armament School at Manby and housed, in addition to the Central Gunnery School, the Junior Weapons School. The aircraft establishment included Meteor 4s and 8s, Spitfire XVIs, Vampire FB Vs, Mosquito 35s, Tempest Vs, Masters, Martinets, Harvards, Lancasters and then the Lincoln. The Flying Wing was commanded by Arthur Donaldson, DSO, DFC, brother of the Air Speed record holder in a Meteor.

One post-war incident worthy of mention concerns the Lincoln from Leconfield which was shot down by Russian fighters in the Berlin corridor, killing the crew.

Light aircraft at Leicester Airport. **Top** *Piper Cherokee Cruiser* G-WOLF *and* **Above** *Cessna 150* G-ECGC.

Leeming, Yorkshire (IV)

In 1984 Royal Air Force Leeming closed for redevelopment which entailed building the hardened shelters to house the Tornado F 3s for the three squadrons that will be formed and housed here. They will take over the duties of the Lightnings at Binbrook.

When the station closed the units from Leeming were either deployed at RAF Scampton or to RAF Linton-on-Ouse. The latter took over the RLG at Dishforth from Leeming.

Leicester East, Leicestershire (II)

The Leicestershire Aero Club, which formed in 1929 with a DH 60 Moth named 'The Quorn', has come a long way since those early days and has a fleet of Cessna 152 and 172 aircraft. The club organises an annual Air Display at the airfield which in 1985 had a record 60,000 people.

Below *Cessna 152* G-BHHJ *and* **Bottom** *Cessna 421* G-BDZU *at Leicester Airport.*

Leighterton aerodrome shortly after the GS hangars were completed. The main accommodation site is to the north near the present 'Aerodrome Garage' (MoD via E.F. Cheesman).

Leicester Airport, known locally as Stoughton Airfield, can accommodate many modern business aircraft. The main runway, Runway 10/28, is tarmac and 994 yd in length. There are also two grass runways suitable for light aircraft when surface winds make the use of the main runway difficult. Hangarage on a permanent or casual basis is readily available and maintenance facilties are provided on request. The hangar houses some 30 privately-owned aircraft. The airfield is fully licenced for commercial charter work.

Leighterton, Gloucestershire

ST829924. 4½ miles SW of Nailsworth alongside A46(T)

A motorist stopping for petrol at the 'Aerodrome Garage' high up in the Cotswolds on the Bath-Stroud main road could be excused for wondering about its name, for it is a pretty unlikely spot for an airfield and there is not one in sight. In fact it is only a mile or so from the World War 2 Babdown Farm, but the garage was in being much earlier and actually derives its name from Leighterton—a flying training station built during 1917 for the Australians.

Leighterton aerodrome opened in February 1918 as No 2 Station of the 1st Wing, Australian Flying Corps, which had its HQ at Tetbury. It was immediately occupied by No 8 (Training) Squadron, AFC, which arrived from Tern Hill via Cirencester on the 18th of the month to provide instruction for embryo fighter pilots using Avro 504K, Pup and Camel aircraft. Five days later No 7(T) Squadron moved in from Yatesbury with Avro 504Ks, BE 2Es and RE 8s to train pilots and observers in the art of Corps recce before posting to Nos 1 and 3 Squadrons, AFC, in France.

The 172-acre field provided adequate landing runs E/W and N/S of 2,700 ft and 3,450 ft respectively, but the height of

An 8 Training Squadron, Australian Flying Corps, Avro 504K outside one of the double GS hangars at Leighterton. The 'emu' badge adorned many of the unit's aircraft (Australian War Memorial).

630 ft above sea level and its exposed position provided plenty of problems for young and inexperienced pilots. The domestic site was at the northern end of the landing ground by Goss Covert while the technical area, which included four 170 ft × 100 ft aeroplane sheds, a similarly sized repair hangar, four stores huts, seven workshops and four MT sheds, lay alongside the A46 opposite the minor road to Boxwell. An air-to-ground range was marked out at Long Newnton two miles to the east (this became an airfield during World War 2—see *Action Stations* 5).

Senior officers lived in Lasborough Park Mansion while their juniors occupied the farm house (now Lasborough Manor House). Local girls were frequent visitors to the aerodrome at weekends and the Australians took part in all local activities with great enthusiasm—doubtless waking up the sleepy Cotswolds in the process!

With typical disregard for authority their aeroplanes were soon gaily painted, No 7(T) Squadron using a boomerang as their unit marking while No 8(T) sported an emu. Individual aircraft often carried additional emblems. Accidents were frequent, the deep ravines just to the west of the aerodrome causing turbulence which made control of flimsy '504s and BE 2Es difficult, though the few DH 6s supplied to No 7 were little better and came in for more contempt, being known as 'butter boxes' because they looked as if they were constructed from ply crates nailed together. All the DH 6s had been withdrawn by August 1918, but the biggest change occurred in October when No 7(T) started to receive the very effective Bristol F 2B and No 8(T) Squadron got some Snipes. By this time an Aircraft Repair Section had been formed at Leighterton, capable of dealing with all the types in use by both Australian training stations (the other was at Minchinhampton), except the Sopwith Snipe which went to No 3 (Western) Aircraft Repair Depot at Yate.

The end of the 1914-18 War saw a rapid run-down though building continued at Leighterton until early in 1919 when contractual difficulties between the Air Ministry and the builders were resolved and work ceased. Limited flying also took place though the air firing range was closed at the end of February when Australian personnel started to leave. They were replaced by No 66 Squadron, RAF, which moved in from Yatesbury during March, joined by No 28 Squadron in June 1919. Both were awaiting demobilisation, No 66 being disbanded on October 25 and No 28 going to Eastleigh to allow the dispersal of Government assets at Leighterton. A large sale was held soon afterwards, most of the buildings being dismantled and re-appearing elsewhere in the district—the NAAFI hut becoming the Richardson Hall at Charfield—the forerunner of the present village hall.

The landing ground was used occasionally during the 1920s and '30s by small private owner aircraft, including those of the Prince of Wales and various Indian Maharajahs who flew in on their way to play polo at country houses in the area. The field was also used by the Bristol Gliding Club, the steep ridge immediately to the west, so awkward for powered aircraft, providing good soaring for their sailplanes.

A more enduring reminder of the airfield, and of the Australians, is provided by an annual memorial service which has been held in Leighterton Church on the first Sunday after Anzac Day ever since 1934—except during the 1939-45 War. It is followed by a parade and wreath-laying

Some of the ex-WD buildings built near Hollom Down Farm as part of the domestic site of Lopcombe Corner are still in good condition.

ceremony in the cemetery—perhaps a unique demonstration of the affection the villagers held for the Australians in general, and the 23 men who lie there in particular.

During the early part of the 1939-45 War a decoy site was laid out at Leighterton. It was bombed on two successive nights, December 15 and 16 1940, without damage to person or property.

A cafe adjoining the 'Aerodrome Garage' uses the old Officers Mess site as an ornamental garden, while more concrete evidence of the airfield is provided by one of the original brick huts, still surviving on the old technical area alongside the busy A46(T).

Leuchars, Fife (VII)

The USAAF Liberators which operated from here in 1944 comprised the 1415th Air Base Unit, European Division of Air Transport Command. Officially classified as 'top secret', the unit had military personnel in civilian clothes and flew passengers and cargo between Leuchars (later from Metfield in Suffolk) and Bromma in Sweden, passing over German-occupied Norway en route. Decoy site for Leuchars was at Craigie. An RAF-flown Puss Moth is reputed to have flown between the twin chimneys of the nearby paper mill!

Lichfield, Staffordshire (III)

No 43 Gliding School re-opened by May 1947 and was active until at least September 1949. There is an interesting and non-standard strongpoint near the old Officers' Mess site, also no less than four mutually supporting pillboxes around the canal bridge on the north-west corner of the aerodrome. No 6 ANS closed December 1953.

Limavady, Londonderry (VII)

No 502 Squadron moved to Docking in Norfolk on January 12 1942. No 224 Squadron went to North Coates, Lincs, on February 18 1942. A detachment of 203 Glidng School flew from here in the early 1950s.

Lindholme, Yorkshire (IV)

In 1985 Royal Air Force Lindholme was bought from the Ministry of Defence for £17.5 million and the Home Secretary announced that the former wartime base would be turned into a Category C prison as an emergency measure to house a soaring number of inmates.

Linton-on-Ouse, Yorkshire (IV)

Royal Air Force Linton-on-Ouse remains the home of Number 1 Flying Training School. This unit provides basic flying training for officers of the Royal Air Force and foreign and Commonweath air forces. After a break of 14 years since Royal Naval officers last trained at Linton-on-Ouse, the first of a continuing series of Sub-Lieutenants RN commenced training in June 1983 with Number 63 Course.

With the anticipation of Leeming's closure for redevelopment, several units began deploying to Linton-on-Ouse on May 23 1983. The MRT at full strength numbers 25 although only five are employed full time for Mountain Rescue duties. The remainder of the team are all volunteers. The team is not just involved in mountain rescue work searching for lost climbers and those involved in accidents. They have also been used as firefighters, cave rescuers and have even provided transport for expectant mothers and sick children in severe weather conditions.

With the closure of Leeming in 1984 the Royal Navy Elementary Flying Training School moved to Linton-on-Ouse. Other units at the station are No 642 Gliding School which trains selected cadets of the Air Training Corps up to solo standard on the Venture T2 motor glider. The Air Training Corps has its North Eastern Regional Headquarters at Linton, as do the Regional Liaison Officers for Numbers 1 and 2 Home Defence Regions.

In August 1983 Linton-on-Ouse handed over the Relief Landing Ground at Elvington to Royal Air Force Church Fenton. The new Relief Landing Ground for Linton is Dishforth, which facility they took over from Leeming. No radical changes are foreseen in the station's future.

Little Sutton, Cheshire (III)

No 192 Gliding School formed here in 1944, and moved to Hawarden in June 1945.

Llanbedr, Gwynedd (III)

No 5 CAACU left in December 1957. The 2025th Gunnery Flight was activated in February 1943 to serve the Atcham fighter training establishment. It moved to Warton on July 6 1943.

Llandow, South Glamorgan (III)

No 614 Squadron was at Cardiff (Pengam Moors) pre-war, not Llandow. In June 1985, one of the 'E' Type hangars on 'D' Site was destroyed by fire.

Llandwrog, Gwynedd (III)

Originally designed as a fighter station in 9 Group. Some 'tidying-up' has taken place here, resulting in the demolition of the original small watch office and some other structures. The tower has been refurbished and a small hangar built for light aircraft. Some of the dispersed sites are still intact and used for light industry. A Seaghull Trench defence structure is built into Dinas Dinlle hill on the airfield approach road.

No 277 MU arrived in September 1946 to run Operation *Dismal*. This was the receipt and disposal of about 9,000 tons of German chemical weapons. The substances were brought by ship to Newport, South Wales, thence by train and lorry to Llandwrog. The unit was later civilianised as a sub-site of 31 MU, Llanberis, and disbanded in September 1953.

Loch Doon, Strathclyde (VII)

At least £600,000 was squandered on this unsuitable site and an aerodrome near Dalmellington, known as Bogton. The Loch was chosen early in 1916 due to its remoteness from habitation and for the hills which descended steeply into the water. These slopes were a necessary feature as rail-mounted targets had to zigzag down the hillside to simulate a manoevring enemy aircraft! The whole scheme was of questionable value and should have been abandoned far sooner than it was. The whole sorry tale is told in fascinating detail in Peter Connon's *An Aeronautical History of the Cumbria, Dumfries and Galloway Region, Part 2: 1915 to 1930.*

Long Kesh, Down (VII)

The reference to 190 Squadron should read 290. Tentatively allocated to the USAAF for an Air Support Command on February 28 1942. Allocated to the 8th Air Force as a bomber training base on August 10 1942 but never occupied by the Americans. Nos 807 and 809 Squadrons formed No 4 Naval Fighter Wing and were equipped with Seafires. The airfield was originally planned to accommodate two medium bomber squadrons and was built partly by Army labour.

Longside, Grampian (VII)

Often known also as Lenabo, Longside housed Coastal and North Sea airships of the Royal Navy to combat U-boats operating against convoys from Scandinavia to the east coast ports. One of the Coastal Airships was believed to have been shot down by a German seaplane and her salvaged propeller is preserved as a memorial in St John's Church, Longside. SSZ airships were also kept at Longside and sometimes operated from clearings in woodlands both near the coast and the coastal convoy route from Aberdeen southwards. The airships made some very long flights; for example, in November 1917 *N511* and *N512* patrolled as far as the Norwegian coast, a return trip of 24 hours. Later, *N512* made a flight of 43½ hours with a southbound convoy from the Orkneys to Stonehaven.

Lopcombe Corner, Hants

SU275356. 8½ miles NE of Salisbury alongside the A30 road

Rather strangely named after the junction between the A30 and A343 roads seven miles south-west of Andover, the 228-acre Lopcombe Corner aerodrome was actually a roughly square piece of open Salisbury Plain grassland about a mile to the east of its namesake. It was built during 1917 as a training station for single-seat fighter pilots and was typical of such a unit. The technical and living sites were on the western edge of the landing ground near Mount Buncas Woods (long since disappeared but then extensive). The main buildings consisted of six aircraft and two storage hangars, an aircraft repair shed and two MT enclosures, plus a large number of wooden huts. In total they covered some 29 acres.

The camp, known locally as Jacks Bush, opened in September 1917 as No 3 Training Depot Station with a very mixed selection of aircraft on strength, BE 2Es and DH 6s being used for initial training while DH 5s and Sopwith Pups were employed for the advanced phases of the course. The thin turf, so typical of the area, was soon cut to ribbons by tailskids which kicked up the chalk base, and Lopcombe became renowned for the mini duststorms created on every take-off in dry weather.

After the formation of the RAF on April 1 1918 the unit operated as part of No 34 Wing, No 8 Group, with an authorised established of 36 Avro 504Ks, 36

Another ex-Lopcombe Corner building alongside the minor road leading from the A30 to Hollom Down Farm.

Sopwith Camels and 839 officers and men. In practice strengths were somewhat different but older aircraft types had been largely weeded out by mid-summer. With the Armistice came the inevitable severe cut-back in flying from Lopcombe and No 3 TDS gradually wound down during the early months of 1919. Some of the released accommodation was used to house personnel of Nos 74 and 85 Squadrons on their return from the Continent during February, the remnants of these units finally dispersing in July.

Air Ministry orders for October 1919 detailed Lopcombe Corner as 'surplus to requirements' and the following month it was closed to aircraft except in an emergency. Preparations for the disposal of buildings and de-requisitioning of the land went ahead, a series of auctions being completed in 1920. A few of the smaller buildings still survive, occupied by small industrial companies near the present-day Hollom Down Farm, on a minor road out of sight from the bustling A30.

Lossiemouth, Grampian (VII)

Mr V.W. Stokes who was with 20 OTU tells me that it was generally accepted that the He 111 on October 26 1940 was not shot down because the gunners had no time to load, the raid was so sudden. From many eyewitnesses the following was more likely: two Heinkels came across the airfeld from east to west in line astern at about 50 ft, the second being caught in the blast from the leader's bombs. Mr Stokes continues: 'A peculiar thing happened following that, a six-wheeled Crossley crash tender headed off towards the Heinkel and went nose down into a bomb crater, its passengers carrying on in a forward path like the Keystone Cops!'

Lough Neagh (Sandy Bay), Antrim

See Sandy Bay.

Luton, Bedfordshire (VI)

TL123210.

Since Volume 6 appeared Luton has seen operations by Boeing 757s and 767s, although 737s still dominate the scene. Britannia Airways, much associated with Luton, operates about 20% of its services from here, and in 1984 the airport handled about 1.8 million passengers, still far short of its huge peaks in the Court days. Still, it remains a very attractive airport and retains a personality so sadly lacking in most such emporiums, but until the nuisance of back-tracking along the 08/26 7,087 ft asphalt runway is cleared Luton will always be handicapped.

Luton is always a busy place, and one of the few where flying takes place every night for from here the Post Office despatches mail to many parts of Europe using Cessna Titans, Trislanders, Bandeirantes, SD 3-30s and so forth. A nightly XP parcels service using F 27s operates to Maastricht in the Netherlands.

On February 25 1985 came the resumption of scheduled services from Luton when London European introduced a regular run to Amsterdam using a Viscount. In eight months 19,000 passengers had availed themselves of the novelty. Then in November 1985 NetherLines opened another link with Amsterdam in pool with London European. The new operator has offered the fascination of travelling on a scheduled service in the increasingly popular 18-seater British Aerospace Jetstream 31.

Lyneham, Wiltshire (VI)

SU007787.

Lyneham remains the home of the RAF's Hercules fleet. Rarely do the 'Herc' squadrons hit the headlines—until disaster strikes the Third World. Then, those sad souls can usually look to Lyneham for some help in their desperate plight. When Mexico City crashed in its 1985 earthquake a Lyneham 'Herc' was soon on the scene. But it is to the pathetic populace of Ethiopia that RAF Hercules crews have, as much as anyone, brought salvation. After at first just moving such supplies as were possible from airfield to airfield while the Marxist air force charged around incompetently, insanely and cruelly snatched people from their homes at gun point, the Lyneham crews were soon switched to air drops of food in frighteningly bumpy conditions and from extremely low levels. No other Air Force equalled them in skill and persistence while at home the folks at Lyneham, knowing only too well of the immense tragedy of Ethiopia, were doing all they could on their own initiative to raise funds. None, it appears, put themselves forward for a New Year's Honour; pride was merely in risking life for others—which is nothing new for the Lyneham folks.

The Hercules C 1K tankers remain in service as such, attached to 24 and 30 Squadrons while crews of 47 and 70 Squadrons usually handle C 1P and C3P aircraft as well as C 1s and C 3s.

Macmerry, Lothian (VII)

Allocated to the 8th Air Force as tactical fighter base on a lodger basis on July 12 1943 but never occupied. No 3 Gliding School formed approximately March 1944 and moved to Drem in the spring of 1946.

Macrihanish, Strathclyde (VII)

Originally known as RNAS Strabane until renamed in June 1941. Nos 821 and 826 Squadrons were present with Fireflies in May 1952 before embarking on HMS *Indomitable.*

Madley, Hereford and Worcester (III)

No 4 RS left for Swanton Morley in November 1946. No 50 Gliding School came here from Hereford Racecourse in January 1946, moving to Pershore in January 1947. The site is now used by British Telecom for satellite communications.

Maghaberry, Antrim (VII)

Tentatively allocated to the USAAF on February 28 1942 for an Air Support Command. Allocated to the 8th Air Force as a transport or observation base on August 10 1942. First occupied by the USAAF in October 1943. Officially transferred to the 8th Air Force on November 15 1943. Transferred to BADA (Base Air Depot Area) in March 1944. Returned to the RAF on June 6 1944. Was at one time to have become the seventh CCRC.

Marham, Norfolk (I)

TF765092.

Marham became the base of the RAF's air-to-air refuelling fleet in 1958. Since 1966 Victor tankers, of which two squadrons, Nos 55 and 57, flying K Mk 2s, have resided here. Training for the AAR role remains the responsibility of 232 Operational Conversion Unit. Many of the Victors, each with around 30 years' service to its credit, wear the hemp and grey colour scheme, and were detached to Ascension's Wideawake airfield during the Falklands' conflict and for months following. Ascension lies 3,900 miles north of Port Stanley, and from the start of Operation 'Corporate', the driving of the Argentine forces from the Falklands, it was clear that any action would involve

Very functional, far from beautiful and drearily painted are the Tornado GR 1s. Cluttered they are with tanks, bombs and pods like 02 *of 27 Squadron, Marham.*

air-to-air refuelling and therefore Marham's Victors. Using those aircraft merely as tankers was seen to waste their potential and so three crews quickly trained, off Scotland, in maritime radar reconnaissance (which duty Wyton's 543 Squadron used to perform) and low-level photography for which purpose cameras had been fitted in the noses of the aircraft whose radio and radar equipment had also been modified.

Early on April 18 1982 an advance party from Marham arrived at Wideawake, followed next day by Victor tankers. The following night the first Victor operation was flown, a night reconnaissance around South Georgia, off the Argentinian coast and over the sea ahead of the Task Force. That entailed an in-flight refuelled operation lasting nearly 14 hours, which was indeed a mammoth effort similarly repeated five times during the course of the following week.

Probably the most spectacular flight involving air-air refuelling took place on the night of April 30 1982 when ten of Marham's Victors and two Vulcans took off from Ascension in two waves for the first bombing of Port Stanley, a five-times refuelled round flight lasting for the Vulcan crews 16 hours.

In-flight refuelling of Nimrods scouring the South Atlantic commenced on May 9, and when on May 16 Hercules transports, with AAR gear fitted at Cambridge (qv), commenced supply drops to the Task Force, these too were refuelled by Marham's Victors. So great was the difference in speed between the Victor and Hercules that refuelling had to take place in a shallow dive. A handful of Hercules tankers was developed to cope with this problem.

The first of the 24 Victor K 2s used at Marham had arrived there on May 7 1974 and served first wth 232 OCU. No 55 Squadron was first to equip with the K Mk 2, followed by 57 Squadron, and both were fully operational by June 1976. The K 2 was superior to the K Mk 1A on account of its longer range, greater fuel lifting capability and increased engine power. Victor K 1As continued in service with 214 Squadron until its disbandment on January 28 1977. The future of Marham's tanker role is in question, for in June 1986 No 57 Squadron disbanded, leaving an enlarged 55 Squadron. The future of AAR clearly lies with the TriStar fleet, for just one TriStar can lift the equivalent fuel load of nine Victors or three VC-10s—and carry ground crew to service aircraft for deployment.

Since *Action Stations 1* appeared Marham has surrendered its Canberra units to Wyton, 100 Squadron leaving in January 1982 and 231 OCU in the middle of that year. Two squadrons new to the station replaced them, Nos 27 and 617, and both operate Tornado GR 1s from the new shelters and supporting complexes situated to the south of the airfield's 9,140-ft-long main 06/24 LCG II runway which has rotary hydraulic arrester gear and is able to accept the heaviest of aircraft. Marham has undergone extensive modifications in recent years although its main update had come in 1944-45 when the main runway was extended to 3,000 yd and the two alternatives to 2,000 yd each.

Tornados arrived first for 617 Squadron re-constituted as the second Tornado GR 1 squadron on January 1 1983 and whose squadron badge is an everlasting reminder of the squadron's fame as 'The

Dam Busters'. Somehow the Tornado, despite its awesome potential, seems unlikely to win the affection and admiration won by its forerunning 'Lancs' and Vulcans. The other Tornado squadron here, No 27 and another ex-Vulcan squadron, established itself during the first half of 1983. It has a long history and performed distinguished overseas service before and during the 1939-45 war. Commonly known as 'The Flying Elephants', the squadron displays that association both in its badge and on its Tornados.

Martlesham Heath, Suffolk (I)

Authority was granted for Martlesham's main runway to be extended to 2,000 yd in the 1950s, for the station was earmarked to accommodate one all-weather fighter squadron—which may explain how the Battle of Britain Flight found itself here, on an 11 Group station. But although the 2,000-yd runway appeared, only 1,800 yd was available for peacetime use. The intention was, during the first five or six weeks of a war, to flatten about 30 houses so that the full runway length could be safely utilised. . . assuming the 'other lot' had not already done even worse.

Maydown, Londonderry (VII)

Built in 1941 by Messrs Cryer & Co. Tentatively allocated to the USAAF for an Air Support Command. Allocated to the 8th Air Force as a fighter base on June 4 1942, but rescinded in April 1943.

Meir, Staffordshire (III)

No 45 Gliding School formed here in August 1942, was redesignated 632 GS in 1955 and was present until at least June 1962.

Merifield, Cornwall

SX33566. 2½ miles WNW of Devonport on minor road off A374

No 16 Balloon Base, No 72 Wing, No 9 Group, was located on the western shore of the Hamoaze, near Merifield (now known as Maryfield). It occupied two small plots totalling 13 acres on land now covered by an enlarged Upper Wilcove village. Six 100 ft × 36 ft Balloon sheds lined the western side of the air station, the technical stores and crew rooms being erected on Looking Glass Point. Domestic accommodation for the 185 personnel of the unit was in HMS *Valiant*, a hulk moored close to the balloon base.

Royal Air Force Melton Mowbray, 14 Recruit Centre, 2 Wing, 'D' Squadron, 16 Flight in the 1950s.

The six operational Kite Balloons, one of which was permanently detached to Berry Head (*SX945565*), were used for convoy protection duties, taken to sea on specially equipped Naval escorts. No 16 Balloon Base commenced operations from both Merifield and a sub-station at RNAS Torquay during 1918, construction work on the parent site being almost complete when the Armistice was declared. After the war the use of Kite Balloons was soon abandoned and Merifield was quickly cleared.

Methwold, Norfolk (I)

Within a few days of Volume 1 appearing about half of the residents of East Anglia were quick to point out that Methwold is in Norfolk and not Suffolk. Apologies; but the misleading postal address for the station was Suffolk, presumably because supplies proceeded there via Brandon railway station? New light upon the station's history shows that Methwold became an airfield before the war, the first aircraft to use the airfield being a Harrow of 37 Squadron which landed on a summer eve possibly in June 1939. Feltwell's operational Wellington squadrons operated at night from Methwold as well as their parent station, indeed 57 Squadron during its long stay generally operated from Methwold. This was mainly to protect the permanent station from damage during intruder attack. In this case the ruse did not work for Feltwell suffered as much as any bomber station from day and night German raids.

Mrs Maisie Gee has thrown light upon the little known Methwold of the period between the withdrawal of the Venturas and the arrival of 3 Group. Following the departure of the squadrons about 22 Americans, believed to be signals personnel, arrived at the station which was then maintained by the RAF Regiment and used as a form of battle school to train RAF aircrew in evading capture, etc, after being shot down. Wimpey, meanwhile, were buildings runways and Lea Valley contractors brought in the ballast. Power Electrical Engineering Works, having dealt with Lakenheath, put in Drem lighting at Methwold. Although some of the wires and cables were temporarily strung among trees, the big switch-on came in May 1944, ready for full-scale bomber 'ops''.

After the war repatriated PoWs were flown to Methwold. As Maisie Gee recalls, 'the aircraft taxied right up to the hangar doors—a lot of swallowing and throat-clearing from the reception committee I can tell you, as we awaited for them to alight. Most were Indian and kissed the ground. They were whisked into a tented enclosure in the hangar and liberally sprayed with DDT powder, going on after registration to a rehabilitation camp at nearby Didlington Park.' Return of these men to their homes was largely undertaken by six East Anglian-based Liberator squadrons.

Middle Wallop, Hampshire (V)

The Museum of Army Flying is now firmly established in a type-design building close to the A343 road and is open daily, except Mondays. The exhibits are well laid out, the flying machines (some of which could not be adequately described as aircraft) being particularly well displayed.

A bonus is the public viewing area adjacent to the museum which overlooks the very active airfield. A weekday visit provides an excellent opportunity to see all the current Army aviation types of helicopter and fixed-wing aircraft at close quarters, as well as providing a fascinating dip into history.

Mildenhall, Suffolk (I)

TL694765.

Basically, Mildenhall remains much as it

One of the mighty 'C' Type hangars at Middle Wallop seen from the public viewing area alongside the excellent Musuem of Army Flying.

Top *Short C-23A Sherpas are busy commuters among USAFE stations.*

Above *C-130 units still rotate to Mildenhall and for several years examples in 'sand tones' were a common sight. One such,* 01260, *is seen here in April 1984.*

was in 1979. The station opened in October 1934 (not 1943 as given in early editions of Volume 1!), and exhibits evidence of several planning changes made during its construction and when it was known as Beck Row. These resulted in two Type 'A' metal hangars being supplemented by three early, non-hipped Type 'C' hangars. Two 1,400-yd concrete runways (040 and 159) were added in 1941-42 and the main one of 2,000 yd. The latter, runway 11/29, was extended post-war to 9,240 ft. Since 1950 Mildenhall has been used by the USAAF. The 513th Tactical Airlift Wing continues to oversee activities by alternately rotated C-130E/H Hercules Wings—the 314th (Little Rock, Arkansas), 317th (Pope, North Carolina) and 463rd (Dyess, Texas)and Airforce Reserve units on 60-day temporary duty here, as they have done since June 1966. It is also the unit responsible for organising the almost daily 60th MAW C-5A and 437th and 438th MAW C-141B cargo supply flights in support of US forces in Britain. Additionally, it controls operations by the Short C-23A Sherpa light transport and feeder liners of the 10th MAS linking US bases in Britain and Europe via Mildenhall. It assists, too, in the handling and support of civilian airliners such as DC 'long 8s' and DC-10s transporting personnel to Europe.

Regularly at Mildenhall are KC-135 tankers of both regular and reserve US forces, their activities controlled still by the 306th Strategic Wing. Quite frequently KC-10 Extenders supplement the KC-135 force.

Autumn 1965 saw the arrival from Chateauroux of three C-118 airborne control aircraft of the 7120 ACCS (Airborne Control & Command Squadron) which in January 1970 became the 10th ACCS. Soon after arrival the squadron re-equipped with half-white EC-135s which have since been repeatedly updated.

U.S. AIR FORCE
WEATHER
50963

80054
U.S. AIR FORCE

10291

Another Wing whose modified Boeing 707s call periodically is the 552nd Airborne Warning Control Wing based at Tinker AFB, and which controls the Boeing E-3A 'AWACS' aircraft. Some 300 C-135 variants have been scheduled to have life extension and CFM-56 engines which greatly quieten the '707' series, and such modified aircraft are seen at Mildenhall.

Also here is Detachment 4 of the 9th Strategic Reconnaissance Wing, Beale, which operates from Mildenhall a fleet of specially adapted KC-135Qs (under the overall control of the 306th Strategic Wing which oversees the tanker operations) whose task it is to refuel Lockheed SR-71As based here. Previously U-2Rs and SR-71s operated under the 306th, before Detachment 4, 9th SRW took command. Since April 1982 an SR-71 has been permanently based at Mildenhall, a second being added late that year. So thirsty is a Mach 3 SR-71 that often during a mission a fleet of tankers positions itself ahead of the Blackbird to refuel it at points along the spy-plane's course. Although the SR-71 is over 20 years old it is still by any reckoning a quite astonishing aeroplane which, when it first appeared, achieved nothing but the unbelievable. So fast and high does it fly that following a typical sortie from Mildenhall it takes half an hour after touch down for the aircraft to cool sufficiently for the crew to climb out. Their flying suits are almost identical to those worn by Space Shuttle crews. Satellite spying—as undertaken over Britain by Russian satellites—has not halted such manned flights which retain high levels of flexibility as well as being conducted with quite astonishing equipment and including relatively conventional cameras.

As well as the SR-71s, Mildenhall fields RC-135s which bristle with aerials and radomes, and which can be used to listen in to, and record radio chatter over sensitive spots at selected times. Since November 1970 such aircraft have been seen here, following the arrival then from Upper Heyford of a detachment of the 98th SRW. In October 1976 the '98th' was placed under the control of the 306th SW which in 1978 moved its headquarters here from Ramstein.

Although by no means a common sight, US Navy aircraft stage through Mildenhall where a small Naval Air Facility remains, operating two Beech UC-12Bs in place of the trusty old Convair C-131s.

No update on Mildenhall can surely overlook mention of its hopefully continuing Air Fête, East Anglia's biggest aeronautical event and probably the best of such shows for it is always packed with interest and never too big to fully digest. Such is its popularity that it usually attracts about half a million visitors! Do they recognise the commentator's voice as that of Roger Hoefling, 'The Voice of Old Warden'?

Milfield, Northumberland (VII)

Hangars today are used as a bulk food store. The former training site is still intact, one of the simulator buildings having blue walls with painted clouds.

Millom, Cumbria (III)

Originally planned for an SFTS. The narrow stubs connecting the runway ends with the perimeter track were known as 'bat handles' and were common to many aerodromes built in the early war period. They were difficult to find at night when taxying off a runway and many were eventually extended to full width when labour became available.

Milltown, Grampian (VII)

No 1674 HCU disbanded here on November 30 1945.

Milmeece, Staffordshire

127/SJ838332.

Commissioned as a camp and ground

Opposite page, top to bottom *Unusual visitors often call at Mildenhall. A typical example is this pale grey WC-130* 50963 *of the 53rd WRS.*

Most of the Mildenhall C-130s are in dreary grey and green camouflage in line with the general toning-down of many aircraft markings in the 1980s.

Backing operations by SR-71 Blackbirds out of Mildenhall is a fleet of KC-135Q tankers, one of which, 80054, *is illustrated.*

Long serving at Mildenhall, a few EC-135s have been repeatedly up-dated, 10291 *among them.*

Corsair at Milmeece for ground training, 1944/45 (Mrs E. Hall).

training school on April 15 1943 as HMS *Fledgling* to train WRNS air mechanics. A number of aircraft were used for ground handling and other practice. Closed after the war but an 'S' Shed and firing butts, plus some huts remain. The site is on the edge of a former shell-filling factory known as Swynnerton, part of which is still occupied by the Army. Close by, just to the west of Stone, was a USAAF depot for replacement aircrew. An ex-Wren told me that its juxtaposition to a camp full of girls was simply asking for trouble!

Minchinhampton (Aston Down), Gloucestershire

SO912012. 1½ miles SE of Chalford on A419.

In 1917 the Australian Flying Corps decided to support their front-line squadrons in France with a training element of their own—in the United Kingdom. The 1st Wing, AFC, was set up with its HQ at Tetbury and after a short period of operation within the RFC training organisation, two new aerodromes in Gloucestershire were handed over to the Australians and their training squadrons renumbered.

No 1 Station of the 1st Wing, AFC, was sited halfway between Stroud and Cirencester and named after the nearby small town of Minchinhampton. Built on 170 acres of comparatively level downland, the field was roughly rectangular giving landing runs of 3,400 ft NW/SE and 2,800 ft SW/NE. The technical site, which consisted of four standard GS sheds of 170 ft × 100 ft, two storage sheds, two workshops and three MT sheds, was built in the

SE 5As of 6 Training Squadron, AFC, at Minchinhampton—some carrying the 'sitting kangaroo' emblem of the unit (Australian War Memorial).

Avro 504Ks in store in one of Minchinhampton's GS hangars—a view showing clearly the construction of the 'Belfast Truss' wooden roof supports (Australian War Memorial).

south-western corner of the airfield while the domestic area was to the north, on the other side of the main road.

No 6 (Training) Squadron, AFC, was the first unit to arrive, moving its Bristol Scouts, Pups and 1½-Strutters in from Tern Hill on February 25 1918. It was joined on April 2 by the MF Shorthorns, DH 6s and Pups of No 5(T) Squadron from Shawbury. Immediately recognisable by the 'sitting kangaroo' markings which embellished the fuselage sides of all No 1 Station aircraft, both units were soon hard at work turning out fighter pilots for the Western Front. Camels joined the original machines, No 5(T) receiving a few two-seaters, while No 6(T) was gradually re-equipped with 25 SE 5As—a most attractive aircraft.

In August 1918 the DH 6 was withdrawn, and with the Shorthorn already replaced the establishment was settled at 12 Camels, 12 SE 5As and 24 Avro 504Ks, though in practice many more were usually on strength. When No 4 Squadron, AFC, started to receive the Sopwith Snipe as the replacement for their Camels in France, a number of these potent new aircraft were added to No 5(T) Squadron's complement. The unit then operated three Flights, 'A' using Avro 504Ks for initial training, 'B' with Pups for intermediate work, and 'C' for advanced instruction using Camels and Snipes.

With the Armistice flying all but ceased at Minchinhampton and Nos 5 and 6(T) Squadrons were disbanded early in 1919, the Australians moving out soon after-

Looking north-east across Minchinhampton aerodrome towards the Stroud-Cirencester road in October 1918. Rows of training aircraft are lined up in front of the temporary canvas hangars (MoD via E.F. Cheesman).

wards. Unusually, no demobilizing RAF squadrons occupied Minchinhampton and it remained almost deserted for most of 1919. To speed up the final disposal of the aerodrome and Air Ministry assets, instructions were issued during November that aircraft were not to land except in emergency. The buildings were auctioned early in 1920 when the site was cleared and returned to farming.

Not for good, however, for the need for more airfields to service the Expansion Schemes of the 1930s resulted in the same site being requisitioned again and it reopened as an ASU/MU during October 1938, renamed Aston Down (see *Action Stations 5*. When Aston Down was extended and runways built the old Stroud-Cirencester road was diverted northwards. The whole of the 1914-18 aerodrome, including the domestic area, lay to the south of the present A419 road.

Molesworth, Cambridgeshire (VI)

Work is well advanced for accommodating 64 Tomahawks of the 550th Tactical Missile Wing which began moving in during 1986. Development of the base will cost around £45 million, NATO and the USA providing £40 million and the British a mere £5 million. The 8½ miles of fencing to keep out the sheep has needed to be duplicated, extra protection being provided for sensitive areas including the missile shelters which are roofed by concrete 16 ft thick.

Without access to highly classified material detailing the Soviet threat and indeed intent, worthwhile opinions on the pros and cons of nuclear defensive systems are impossible to formulate. I was standing close to a Russian leader when he assaulted us with the menacing, 'We will bury you', a chilling experience which I shall never forget nor forgive, for clearly he meant it. The 550th gives his successors something to ponder over.

Mona, Anglesey (III)

Originally planned as a fighter station in 9 Group. No 63 Gliding School, which had formed at Tal-y-Cafn, south of Conway, around October 1943, came to Mona in June 1946 and stayed at least six months.

Montford Bridge, Shropshire (III)

'MB' is still painted on the roof of the tower. No 34 MU continued breaking up aircraft until July 1947 when it moved to Sleap. Most were Masters but a Typhoon 1b was flown in from Defford early in 1946 for attention. Some of the Masters were reprieved and flown out to Miles Aircraft at Woodley for overhaul as target tugs. A canvas Bessonneau hangar was erected for the MU's use.

Montrose, Tayside (VII)

The original Montrose aerodrome was sited at Upper Dysart beside the A92 about three miles south-west of the town. Montrose had been an important centre for military training since 1850 and it was thus a logical step to locate early Scottish military flying close to an existing barracks. Dysart was never more than a tented camp with canvas hangars and existed for only about 12 months. A better site at Broomfield was found and operations were moved there. A landing ground known as Dysart was used by Montrose aircraft in the 1930s but was, however, on a different site. (The date on the petrol bill illustration on page 156 of Volume VII is April 14 19*14*.)

Montrose is now a centre for microlight flying. Two of the First World War hangars have been dismantled and reerected at the railway museum at Bo'ness on the north bank of the Firth of Forth.

Moreton, Dorset

SY762898. 4½ miles E of Dorchester off minor road.

A late starter in the chain of airship stations along the south coast of England, Moreton was intended to plug an embarrassing gap in convoy coverage off the south coast. 355 acres of low-lying pasture bounded on the south by the Dorchester-Wareham railway line and to the north by the grounds of Woodsford Castle was chosen and construction of airship sheds, workshops and a gas plant was started during 1918. It was not very far advanced when the Armistice was signed and work at Moreton ceased immediately.

Seventeen years later, with the first of the Expansion Schemes in full flood, a survey team checked the old airship station's suitability as an aerodrome, but they finally chose a site immediately to the south on Woodsford Heath, presumably because of better drainage. Opened as Woodsford Armament Practice Camp it was later renamed Warmwell, and had no connection with Moreton (which took its name from a village 2½ miles to the east).

The Moreton site was largely cleared soon after the 1914-18 War but a number

Dispersal area at Morpeth with Blister hangar to right (F. Neal).

of the buildings still survive and the track running westward out of High Woodsford village owes its foundations to the uncompleted airship station.

Mount Batten, Devon (V)

During 1984 it was announced that the RAF Marine Branch would be disbanded on April 1 1986, and that its main base at Mount Batten would then be closed. The Marine Craft Training School arrived at Mount Batten in 1953 and was joined by the School of Combat Survival & Rescue in 1959 and No 2 (County of Devon) Maritime HQ, Royal Auxiliary Air Force, the following year. Presumably the RAuxAF unit will move across the Cattewater to Mount Wise, and the SofCS&R will migrate to another station with easy access to the combination of rugged moorland and the sea so necessary for survival training—and which made Mount Batten so ideal.

It is unlikely that Mount Batten will be

Cattewater (Mount Batten) with a long row of Short 184 floatplanes on the pier in 1918. Note the rail-mounted crane which lifted the machines in and out of the water (RAF Mountbatten).

Above *Mullion Airship Station with construction of the second shed just beginning. The large, and very necessary, wind breaks are clearly visible. The main domestic area is located around the small wood to the north of the hangars* (FAA Museum, A/Stn 136).

Below *Both airship sheds at Mullion are now complete and aircraft of the Special Duty Flights making up 236 Squadron are also in evidence* (Osborne Studios).

Bottom *The* SS 27 *at Mullion over the canvas Bessoneaux hangars of 236 (Landplane) Squadron. One of the huge wind breaks is just visible on the right of the photograph* (via M. Hodgson).

entirely relinquished by the MoD, and even more unlikely that it will again become the popular rendezvous it was for Plymothians before the 1914-18 War. Then day trippers crossed from the Barbican to enjoy the fresh air and to visit the fairground, side shows, food stalls and pub which were then on the narrow peninsula. In 1917 the 'Castle Inn' became the first station commander's residence, and the 14 cottages clustered round it were demolished to make room for wooden huts—Mount Batten was never quite the same again!

Mullaghmore, Londonderry (VII)

Allocated to the 8th Air Force as bomber training base on August 10 1942, Mullaghmore was officially transferred to the 8th on December 20 1943 then to Services of Supply in March 1944 and back to the RAF on May 1 1944.

Mullion, Cornwall

SW705210. 2 miles NE of Mullion village, off the A3083.

His Majesty's Airship *C9*, a Coastal type craft, left Mullion at 05.05 hours on June 22 1917 for a patrol off Start Point. At 07.30, when about 15 miles south of the Point, a light green-coloured shape was observed beneath the sea surface. Bubbles and a fine oil emulsion were rising from it, but it appeared stationary. HM Destroyer *73*, patrolling to eastward, was signalled and requested to investigate but when the ship was still some three miles away the object moved off at about five knots to the north-west leaving a trail of oil about 300 ft long. As the destroyer closed the quarry stopped again—it was obviously a submarine.

The airship's pilot, Flight Commander J.G. Struthers, RN, aimed a 65-lb delayed action bomb at the middle of the green shape and the destroyer immediately moved in and dropped two depth charges within 20 ft of the U-boat. Some wreckage and oil came to the surface and bubbles continued to rise for some time. There is little doubt that the submarine had been waiting for a convoy of eight ships which approached Prawle three hours later, but with no further sighting and worsening weather the *C9* was recalled at 11.25. In thunder and heavy rain she struggled back to Mullion against strong winds, finally landing at 15.55. The Lizard Wireless Station reported the U-boat being called by her base for several hours without response, but there was no positive proof of her destruction so no claim could be entertained—a common feature of anti-submarine warfare.

The German declaration of a submarine blockade of Britain made early in 1915, and the sharply increased shipping losses which followed, posed a serious threat. Part of the solution lay in the extension of airship patrols westwards, and this meant the establishment of bases in the West Country. The Lizard Peninsula was a natural choice for such a base and it was not long before a suitable site was chosen on rough downland between Mullion and Garras, close to the extensive Bonython plantation.

At first known as the Lizard Airship Station, the 320-acre site was soon cleared and work started on a large shed, 300 ft long, 100 ft wide and 70 ft high, workshops and a hutted camp, the still incomplete station being commissioned as RNAS Mullion during June 1916. The first airship sent to Mullion was the *C8*, one of the very successful 'Coastal' type developed from the SS (Sea Scout). She left Kingsnorth on June 8 but never reached her destination, coming down in the Channel off Start Point with the loss of three of her crew, only the wireless operator being picked up. This tragedy resulted in the next two Coastals being despatched by rail and road, but they were quickly assembled, the first test flight from Mullion being made on June 18, with *C9* making the first of many patrols on July 1.

Operations were uneventful until September 9 1916 when the crew of *C10* sighted two small vessels on fire off the Lizard. As they closed to investigate a U-boat was seen but it dived before they could mount an attack. Soon after the destroyer *Foyle* reached the scene the submarine re-appeared, only to submerge again when engaged by the warship's guns. No claim could be made but the crew of *C10* had the satisfaction of knowing they had made the first U-boat interception by a RNAS airship—and that they had driven it off.

Flown as usual by Flight Commander J.G. Struthers, the *C9*'s first tussle with the enemy was in February 1917 when an underwater trail was detected. A bomb was dropped and naval trawlers called in, the latter bringing up wreckage but nothing conclusive.

A portable shed joined the original airship hangar during February 1917 and these increased facilities allowed patrols to be started off the north Cornwall coast. On April 3 Mullion became part of the re-organised 'South Western Group' which had its HQ in Plymouth, one of the first obvious changes being the arrival of four Sopwith 1½-Strutters to relieve the hard-pressed airships of inshore patrol work. For the greater part of 1917 only two of the latter, the *C9* and *C22*, were available and the Strutters flew from an improvised landing ground at Mullion until August 1917 when they were withdrawn to fill gaps in France following heavy losses on the Western Front.

The *C9* continued in the forefront of the activity at Mullion, attacking another submarine in June 1917, and yet another on September 21 after the French steamer *Rouang* had been torpedoed off the Lizard. After spending five hours in the area waiting for the stricken ship to be taken in tow, the crew of *C9* sighted the conning tower of a submarine moving towards a Falmouth-bound convoy. Struthers attacked it with two 100-lb bombs and was rewarded with a violent explosion, quantities of air and some oil. The *C2* and *C23* took over the search, joined by surface vessels, and the next day the oil patch covered a considerable area —*C9* and her crew were credited with a 'probable'. Seven days later, on September 29, the *C9* was involved in more excitement when the crew observed submarine tracks near the Eddystone lighthouse and co-operated with depth-charging trawlers by dropping a flare and a bomb. Again large quantities of oil came to the surface. Unfortunately Struthers could not await developments because the *C9* had already been airborne for 11 hours and was 60 miles downwind of Mullion— so he had to leave the hunt to the surface forces.

Not all crews were so successful and even to survive the dangers inherent in such operations required an element of luck. The patrol by the *SSZ14* which started at 09.00 hours on September 7 under the command of Flight Lieutenant Elliott was such a case. It was uneventful until 16.25 when the engine suddenly stopped and could not be restarted. In a freshening wind the disabled 'ship' was blown steadily out to sea and equipment had to be jettisoned to prevent a ditching. At last the *SSZ14* drifted over the French coast and at 21.15 it touched down heavily on Cap Finisterre. The crew scrambled out and managed to deflate the envelope. The damaged craft was taken to the French base at Guipas, repaired, re-inflated, and on September 21 crew and 'ship' returned triumphantly to Mullion.

The south-westerly gales which often swept the approaches to the English Channel were particularly hazardous for airships, both on patrol and at base, though at Mullion the effect of gusty conditions was diminished when wind breaks were built at the ends of the airship sheds. One such gale nearly ended the career of *C9*, the 'Darling of the Airship Service', on October 3 1917. Following a weather recall she was on her way back when Flight Commander Struthers saw an explosion amongst six ships off Bolt Head, some six miles astern. Swinging the airship around he was overhead 2½ minutes later, in time to see the residual track of a torpedo—and at the end of it the outline of a submarine. Bombs were dropped and patrol vessels homed in before Struthers turned for home. He arrived perilously short of fuel after taking six hours to cover 40 miles in the teeth of a gale.

During 1917 Mullion had been the most active of the airship stations, 2,845 operational hours being flown on convoy escorts and in co-operation with surface craft. Early in 1918 it became even busier when landplanes returned following the revival of the inshore patrol scheme. This time they were DH 6 biplanes, a rather unsatisfactory machine only effective because the sight of any aeroplane kept U-boats submerged. In May Nos 515 and 516 (Special Duty) Flights were joined by No 493 Flight which had the much more effective DH 9 light bomber, and during August 1918 the three Flights formed the components of No 236 Squadron, RAF, as part of the 71st Wing, No 9 (Operations) Group. By this time six Bessoneaux hangars had been erected near the Plantations, the additional personnel living in tents and Armstrong huts.

Meanwhile, the Mullion airships had undertaken hydrophone trials using the codename 'Rubber Eel'. By September the results were considered promising enought to warrant general introduction aboard all 'Zero' non-rigids—but it was to be another 27 years before airborne acoustic equipment became a practical anti-submarine device.

The famous *C9* was deflated for the last time on September 14 1918 after two years' and 75 days' service at Mullion, during which she flew an astonishing

3,720 hours. All the 'Coastals' were in poor shape by this time and at the Armistice only *C2* remained at Mullion alongside seven SSZs and a single SS Twin. By the end of November all were deflated except the Mullion Twin, known locally as the 'Silver Queen', which made the last airship ascent from Mullion on January 25 1919. The landplanes were still in desultory operation until March 1919, No 236 Squadron officially disbanding on May 15 when the RAF decided to rely exclusively on flying boats for peacetime maritime duties.

The airship stations, Mullion included, were soon abandoned. The Bessoneaux hangars and tents were quickly removed, followed by the airship sheds and installations. Just one or two buildings were left to be be used during World War 2 by personnel of an experimental balloon station formed on the site—and by airmen from the nearby Chain Home radar unit at Drytree. The foundations of roadways and windbreaks are still visible today, slowly mouldering away in the shadow of Goonhilly satellite station.

Newlyn, Cornwall

SW468281. 2 miles S of Penzance on minor road.

On a narrow strip of reclaimed land between Newlyn harbour and Carn Gwavas the RNAS base of Newlyn (Lands

Below *A bombed-up Short 184 floatplane at Newlyn in May 1918. The chapel in the background has recently been transformed into an attractive private dwelling* (P. Liddle via G.S. Leslie).

Bottom *The Bessoneaux hangars and a Short 184 at RNAS Newlyn in October 1918* (B. Robertson).

Hunter F 4—gate guardian at RAF Newton in May 1983.

End) was opened early in 1917 when seaplane patrols were first extended into the south-west approaches.

Protection from the weather for the Short seaplanes which equipped the unit was first provided by Bessoneaux canvas hangars and, apart from a hardstanding above the north facing slipway, facilities were spartan in the extreme. 'York House' was hired as accommodation for officers, ratings living in two other requisitioned houses in the vicinity. As the size of the unit increased a 180 ft × 60 ft seaplane shed was built at the southern end of the base area to house the six floatplanes (mainly Short 184s) on strength at the end of 1917. It was one of these excellent machines which made the first attack launched from Newlyn—bombing a submarine south-west of the Lizard during December.

Newlyn had also been discovered by the crews of Scilly-based aircraft, the Curtiss H 12 'Large America' *8652* landing there with engine trouble on March 11 1917, damaging its tail in the process. Its companion, *8654*, arrived early in May after getting lost in fog, and ten months later, on March 3 1918, another drama occurred. An American pilot based at Newlyn, Ensign Benjamin Lee, and his observer, Sub-Lieutenant Rowley, RNAS, got lost while patrolling the Lands End area aboard Short 184 *N1606*. In poor weather and approaching darkness they finally reached the Eddystone lighthouse and after circling it put down on the water nearby. They tried to taxy into the lee of the rocky outcrop, but hit it and shattered both floats. The attention of the lighthouse keepers had been attracted and they managed to get a lifebuoy to Lee, risking their lives to haul him on to the base of the lighthouse. Unfortunately the observer was lost, but the rescue of anyone from the seas around the Eddystone using nothing but a lifebuoy and brawn is an extraordinary achievement, marked by a well-deserved letter of commendation from the Secretary of the US Navy to the keeper, J.F.W. Williams.

Following the formation of the RAF in April 1918 the seaplane bases were reorganised, and in May the aircraft at Newlyn were divided between two Flights, Nos 424 and 425, each nominally established with six Short 184s. Strengths, however, were much lower, only three floatplanes being available at the beginning of July, though the situation did improve later in the month.

The Newlyn floatplanes co-operated with flying boats from the Scillies, and airships from Mullion (and its substations), to provide continuous cover for convoys moving in and out of the English Channel. This work, like all maritime patrol operations, was usually uneventful, the monotony only rarely interrupted by sudden action like the attack on a suspicious oil slick by the crew of Short *N1770* on July 13 1918. Renewed U-boat

Varsity WL627 *at Newton in May 1983.*

The arrival from the United States of a Thor missile brought in by a USAF Cargomaster to North Luffenham in March 1960.

activity during the spring and early summer of 1918 resulted in a fresh spate of emergency diversions by Scilly-based Short seaplanes, two of which were towed in after landing out at sea with engine trouble, while on June 19 another H 12 landed in Mounts Bay after running out of fuel. Newlyn personnel also developed a certain expertise for salvaging DH 6 coastal patrol aeroplanes from the sea—their engines were notoriously unreliable.

In August 1918 No 235 Squadron was formed at Newlyn to control and coordinate the activities of the two Flights, operating as part of No 71 Wing, Penzance. A number of Short 320 floatplanes arrived to supplement the '184s and a handful of Sopwith Baby seaplanes have also been reported at Newlyn at this time. The latter certainly did not stay long and with the Armistice activity rapidly declined, No 235 Squadron being disbanded on February 22 1919. Newlyn was soon abandoned, but retained on the Air Ministry emergency base list. It was visited by the Seaplane Development Flight in August 1922 during their south coast cruise, much excitement being caused by the arrival of the Short Cromarty, a Porte F3, a Kingston and the Lion-engined Porte F5 from Cattewater, Plymouth. They made an impressive sight moored off the coast, but were shortly on their way to the Scillies, and Newlyn was soon deleted from the emergency list having been declared unsuitable for large flying boats.

During the 1920s the wooden pier which had formed the seaward side of the RNAS base, and from which seaplanes had been launched, was destroyed in a storm—the slipway disappeared later. Newlyn made another name for itself during World War 2, however, becoming the home of a RAF Air Sea Rescue unit which featured in some spectacular operations, saving over 100 aircrew using high-speed launches.

The site of the RNAS base is now used by ARC Southern Ltd as a storage area for locally quarried granite.

Newtownards, Down (VII)

The reference to Ballykelly in connection with 1493 Flight should read Ballyhalbert. Airfield allocated to the 8th Air Force for observation units on August 10 1942. Allocation rescinded on August 27 1942 as location too far away from other 8th Air Support Command bases.

North Weald, Essex (VIII)

North Weald lives on and could become the leisure airfield of the future—the Fighter Meet and the North Weald Restoration Flight is a fine example to make this possible. The flight has established a museum relating to the airfield and its collection of aircraft includes a Sopwith Pup, DV Albatross, BE 2C, Percival Proctor V, cockpit sections of a Canberra B 2 and Hunter F 4. There is Also a D4 Link Trainer and various engines.

Many buildings of this famous airfield remain almost intact and North Weald will never be forgotten. On Remembrance Day wreaths are laid at a monument near the main entrance. This monument was unveiled on June 19 1952 by HRH Princess Astrid on behalf of the Norwegian Fighter Squadrons which had fought from North Weald. The inscription on the monument reads: 'Dedicated, in gratitude, to the Royal Air Force, to the Royal Air Force Station North Weald and to the people of the District'.

The intention of Epping Forest District Council is to retain the wartime airfield of North Weald as a leisure facility. The 380-acre site is located close to the intersection of the M11 and M25 motorways and is also served by London Regional Transport underground line. There are

Old Sarum in September 1918. Compare with the 1956 photograph in Action Stations 5—*remarkably little change occurred over the intervening 40-odd years* (P. Liddle via G.S. Leslie).

many air activities and on the ground the airfield hosts several sports such as pistol shooting and gymnastics. The former aircraft hangars that once housed Spitfires and Mustangs are now used for commercial warehousing.

Nutt's Corner, Antrim (VII)

Tentatively allocated to the USAAF for an Air Support Command on February 28 1942. Allocated to the 8th Air Force as a bomber training base on August 10 1942. Transferred to the RAF on January 12 1943 for Ferry Command.

Oakington, Cambridgeshire (I)

Oakington was an active airfield for nearly 30 years after the war, and was earmarked in the 1950s as Waterbeach's standby for its fighters and listed as a V-bomber dispersal airfield. The buildings remain, and in good health, but Oakington's airfield status has been much reduced. After the Army moved in during 1975 Oakington's costly-to-maintain landing ground underwent dramatic change. Trees and shrubs were planted in groups on the flying field and almost the whole main runway was removed, leaving a short section at its east end. But flying is far from over for a dozen helicopters of 657 Squadron Army Air Corps are very active from their Oakington home.

On October 1 1969 No 665 Squadron re-formed at McMunn Barracks, Colchester, taking over six Scouts and six Sioux helicopters previously in the hands of the 19th Flight AAC working with the 1st Battalion, Prince of Wales' Own Regiment, and the Air Troop, 1st Regiment Royal Horse Artillery. The squadron, renumbered 657 on April 1 1978, moved here in January 1979 because it was earmarked as a Lynx anti-tank squadron whose aircraft would have been too noisy and large to have been accommodated at Colchester Barracks. Half the squadron flies Lynx AH 1s armed with TOW missiles while the remainder flies Gazelles (first received in February 1978) whose role is one of tank spotting. Rotation of Army Air Corps squadrons to the Falklands includes No 657, but its Lynx heli-

The DH 6s of 250 Squadron lined up at Padstow (Crugmeer) late in 1918 (Mrs E.M.V. Buckingham, Padstow).

Top *Ouston tower, a modified 518/40 design, in 1983.*

Above *Nestling close up to Crugmeer village are the tents and hangars of Padstow aerodrome in 1918. Eleven DH 6/DH 9 aircraft and the line of removed Cornish dry walls are clearly visible* (P. Liddle via G.S. Leslie).

Below *Army Lynx helicopters operate from the ASP at Oakington where Varsities used to roam.* XZ221 *is depicted.*

copters remain here and in the southern outpost it flies Gazelles and Scouts with which types the squadron was armed when it moved to Oakington.

Oban, Strathclyde (VII)

No 228 Squadron left for Castle Archdale on December 11 1942.

Old Sarum, Wiltshire (V)

Old Sarum was reprieved at the last minute, this time by a new aircraft manufacturer with a very original product—the extraordinary-looking Edgley Optica. Negotiations for the purchase of the airfield and some of the First World War GS hangars commenced in 1981 and it was not long before construction of a prototype aircraft was underway. Ambitious plans for an initial batch of 200 Opticas were made, and by August 1984, when the first production aircraft flew, some 80 were said to be on the order book. Since then Edgley Aircraft Ltd has gone into receivership but Alan Haikney purchased the company in December 1985 and, renamed Optica Industries Ltd, production resumed during 1986.

The reason for the sudden move of 43 OTU to Oatlands Hill in February 1944 is now known. Old Sarum was needed as a maintenance depot for vehicles destined for use during the D-Day landings. The hangars were cleared and used to put vehicles through a 'SNUG' process which enabled them to be driven ashore from Landing Craft Tank (LTC) or Landing Ship Tank (LST). The work included the blanking off of all holes except those needed for breathing, and the fitting of flexible pipes to carburettors and exhausts to keep such intakes/outlets above water. Sandbags were placed on the floor of vehicles to reduce the risk of injury to driver's legs from exploding mines. The modifications were made on a 'production-line' principle, vehicles being driven through the hangars by personnel of RAF Servicing Commando units who also took part in the work schedules. On completion the trucks were dispersed in fields around the airfield and the personnel settled into camps to await D-Day. It was part of the massive build-up in the south of the country during the early months of 1944 —and a triumph of logistics and planning.

Ollerton (Hinstock), Shropshire

See Hinstock.

Ouston, Northumberland (VII)

No 27 Gliding School moved in from Woolsington in June 1948. Redesignated 641 GS around August 1955.

Padstow (Crugmeer), Cornwall

SW898765. 1½ miles NW of Padstow off minor road.

With the Admiralty decision to extend coastal anti-submarine coverage westwards early in 1918, suitable sites for landing grounds in north Cornwall and Devon became a priority. One of those finally authorised was close to the hamlet of Crugmeer. It was tentatively named Trevose Head, chosen more for its position than the quality of the ground which consisted of a number of steeply sloping fields not far from the cliff top.

With the Cornish dry stone walls cleared away, the 50 acre LG provided a 1,500-ft landing run into the prevailing wind, adequate for lightly loaded biplanes despite the adverse slope. Four Bessoneaux hangars and a MT shed were built and the field opened as Padstow/Crugmeer in March 1918. It was operational by the end of the month, the 12 DH 6 coastal patrol aeroplanes being split into two sections which became Nos 500 and 501 Flights on May 31. A small number of Curtiss JN-4 Jenny (another under-powered ex-trainer) biplanes were also used but these had gone by the time the six DH 9s of 494 Flight were fully established on the LG in mid-June. The personnel, now totalling some 180, lived uncomfortably in tents or locally hired buildings in the teeth of the frequent gales which afflict this unprotected headland facing out into the Atlantic.

In August 1918 the Flights came under the newly formed No 250 Squadron, RAF, which established its HQ at Padstow and operated as part of No 71 Wing, No 9 Group, Plymouth. Already the LG had been found to be one of the more difficult to fly from, especially for pilots of the Curtiss OX-5-engined DH 6s. With bombs aboard they were often unable to climb over the cliffs on return, and were forced to fly up a conveniently positioned valley just south of Gunver Head, though turbulence could make this practice extremely hazardous.

During their lonely two-hour patrols the DH 6 pilots rarely saw any sign of the enemy, but it was noticeable that shipping was only attacked when travelling unescorted along the north Cornish coast

—such occasions being confined to periods of westerly gales and sea fog when flying from Padstow was virtually impossible. One of the few U-boat sightings by the coastal patrol organisation was made by Lieutenant Shorter from a 250 Squadron DH 6 during August 1918, but his elation was short-lived for both his bombs failed to explode.

After the Armistice little flying was done but the LG remained open until the end of March 1919 and No 250 Squadron was not disbanded until May 15. The landing ground was quickly returned to agriculture and RNAS/RAF Padstow was soon just a memory—though a vivid one for some Padstonian matrons!

During World War 2 a radio station was built on the site and a number of Maycrete buildings erected, some of which are now used for farming purposes.

Pembrey, West Glamorgan (III)

No 5 Squadron left in October 1949. No 233 OCU formed here in September 1952 and closed in May 1957. Chiefly used Meteors and Vampires.

Pembroke Dock, Dyfed (III)

Two 'A'-type hangars and a 'T2' still exist, the latter in use by the Royal Navy. No 4 OTU arrived from Alness in August 1946, later becoming 235 OCU and leaving for Calshot in February 1949. A memorial was dedicated during 1985.

Pengam Moors (Cardiff), South Glamorgan (III)

No 3 RFS formed here in August 1948 and closed in July 1953. No 614 Squadron formed here on June 1 1937 (not at Llandow) and moved to Odiham on October 2 1939. No 3 RFS formed in August 1948 and closed in July 1953. As a footnote, there were two US Army strips for Cub-type aircraft within the Cardiff city limits in 1944.

Penkridge, Staffordshire (III)

The wartime site plan shows Blister hangars so the Robins here today possibly came from the nearby Teddesley Park SLG.

Penrhos, Gwynedd (III)

On the steep little hill overlooking the technical site many gorse-covered defences works can be found. They include some unusual double pillboxes, AA posts and sheltered accommodation for the gun crews. The Battle HQ is so overgrown as to be almost invisible and near it, on the highest point of the ridge, is an obstruction light pole complete with original fittings. On a dispersed site is a Blister hangar once used to house a free gunnery trainer. On closer examination it appears that there is no post-war light aircraft strip, a private owner merely uses a stretch of the old perimeter track.

AM Bombing Trainer building at Peplow.

Peplow (Childs Ercall), Shropshire (III)

A bombing trainer building survives, along with an unusual operations block.

Pershore, Worcester and Hereford (III)

No 1 Ferry Unit moved to Manston on May 17 1948. No 50 Gliding School arrived from Madley in January 1947 but suspended operations on June 1 1948. The RAF Police Training School was present 1948-51. No 10 AFS, which formed here in 1952, disbanded in 1956. Long Marston was used as a satellite.

Perton, West Midlands (III)

First used from September to November 1941 as a RLG for 28 EFTS, Wolverhampton. The airfield was transferred to Army Co-operation Command from April to May 1942 for reasons unknown. It was still in use as a satellite of Seighford by 21 PAFU in the summer of 1946. The unit of the Royal Netherlands Army present in 1941 was the *Princes Irene* Brigade. The tower still stands and has been used variously as a doctor's surgery and as a local community centre. A memorial stone has been placed nearby noting that this was once an aerodrome.

Peterborough (Westwood), Cambridgeshire (VI)

A reference on page 52 of Volume 6 to Westley should of course refer to Westwood from where in 1969, according to David Benfield, a Bellman hangar was taken to Sibson for club use. Sibson, he correctly points out, never passed beyond the grass runway stage with the present club airfield being built north of the old airfield boundary.

It is perhaps worth adding that Peterborough has long been associated with flying for Sage & Co of Walton built Short Seaplanes, Avro 504Ks and prototypes of their own designs before the 1914-18 war ended. Their premises were bought in 1936 by the Aeronautical Corporation of Great Britain in order to build the American-designed Aeronca C-3. It was not a success and the works closed late in 1937.

Peterhead, Grampian (VII)

The squadron which re-formed here on July 7 1941 was 132 not 143.

Polebrook, Northamptonshire (VI)

A post-war intention was to develop Polebrook as an RAF bomber base, but eventually Molesworth was substituted—hence its survival. The Thor missiles based here were with 130 Squadron which formed December 1 1959 and disbanded on August 23 1963, these dates also being applicable to 218 Squadron (also Thor-equipped) at Harrington, Northamptonshire.

Port Ellen, Strathclyde (VII)

On January 20 1942 the CO of 134 Squadron, Eglinton, visited Port Ellen to investigate the possibility of operating from here because of the muddy conditions at Eglinton.

Spitfire of 164 Squadron at Peterhead in 1942 (R.E.G. Sherward via C.H. Thomas).

Portland, Dorset (V)

The introduction of the Lynx helicopter as a replacement for the Wasp on all but the smallest frigates has resulted in considerable changes at Portland in recent years. No 703 Squadron was re-absorbed by 829 in January 1981 and in August 1982 the latter unit also took over parenting of the few remaining Wessex 3 ship-borne Flights from 737 Squadron. Despite this move 737 Squadron continued training replacement crews for the aircraft until disbanded on February 7 1983. By this time 829 Squadron was concentrating on the gradually dwindling number of Wasp-equipped Flights aboard ship, the HQ Flight at Portland also being responsible for all training on the type.

Meanwhile, the Lynx-equipped 702 and 815 Squadrons had moved from Yeovilton to Portland on July 19 1982, the former providing pilot/observer conversion and operational training on the new helicopter while 815 parented the rapidly expanding number of Ships' Flights operating the aircraft. Both units operate the basic HAS 2 and updated HAS 3 versions of the Lynx.

By 1985 the Portland scene had again stabilised with the two Lynx units, 702 and 815 Squadrons, the Wasps of 829 and the Wessex HU 5s of 772 Squadron on strength. It remains a busy place well worth visiting on 'Air Days'.

Porton Down, Wiltshire

SU205365. 5 miles NE of Salisbury.

Opened as a bombing range in 1920, Porton Down was used by aircraft of the Wessex Bombing Area but gradually became increasingly associated with the Chemical Defence Establishment and its gas spraying and smoke-laying trials. One of the earliest aircraft used for these experiments was a specially-equipped Fairey IIIF.

A landing ground was laid out alongside the range and was used widely by Army Co-operation machines during exercises, Audax and Hector biplanes being frequent visitors during the late 1930s. By 1939 it was apparently in the hands of the Army, but when the A&AEE moved into nearby Boscombe Down at the beginning of World War 2 Porton was pressed into service for weapon trials whilst new specialist ranges were completed. Work then concentrated on chemical warfare testing, some very bizarre schemes being tried out as well as more practical 'bread and butter' items like the development of large-scale smoke screens to cover landings of airborne troops—this was first demonstrated at Porton on September 10 1941. Aircraft belonging to the CDES Porton, but based at Boscombe, also provided gas attack training for courses at Rollestone until late 1942—and probably throughout the war.

Always a secretive place, Porton maintained a very low profile during the war, and the crash of a Whitley V of No 138 Squadron on the range during the early hours of April 21 1942 must have caused quite a flap. It was returning from a *Nickelling* operation at very low altitude and ploughed into rising ground near Battery Hill, killing the four-man crew.

Though little used after the war, the LG was retained until 1949, and was again in action during 1956 when Auster Autocar *G-ANVN/XJ941* of the Colonial Insecticide Research Unit tested its chemical spray attachments before going out to Malaya. Eight years later the Whirlwind 7 *XG589* was transferred to the MoA for research work by the Civil Defence Experimental Establishment at Porton—though it spent much of its time at the A&AEE Boscombe Down until withdrawn in November 1971.

On April 1 1979, after Britain had renounced the use of chemical warfare, the Microbiological Research Establishment, Porton Down, was transferred from the MoD to the Public Health Laboratory Service Board. The Secretary of State for Social Services took over ministerial responsibility for the unit which presumably continues work on means of combating 'warfare' gases and liquids in addition to more mundane trials. Although now a considerably less sensitive place than in earlier years, the Establishment is still surrounded by signs discouraging stopping or loitering.

Portsmouth, Hampshire (IX)

During 1984-85 the destruction of the aerodrome and the old Airspeed factory gathered pace, a 90-acre site being redeveloped as part of a £40-million scheme which will create 700 houses, a shopping and community centre plus an enlarged industrial estate.

Prawle Point, Devon

SX778368. 3 miles SE of Salcombe on minor road.

An upsurge in German submarine activity

in the south-west approaches to the English Channel early in 1917 soon overstretched the available flying boats, seaplanes and airships. To relieve them of inshore patrol work the Admiralty decided to allocate 12 Sopwith 1½-Strutters for this work. Headlands were quickly surveyed for suitability as landing grounds, one of those chosen being a 50-acre site immediately to the west of East Prawle village, and roughly rectangular in shape.

The LG was opened in April 1917 with the minimum of facilities necessary to operate four 1½-Strutters, both men and machines being provided with tented accommodation. The detachment, and similar ones at Mullion and Pembroke, was successful but the insatiable demand for pilots to replace losses on the Western Front forced withdrawal of the units during August.

Prawle Point, as the LG was called, lay dormant but not forgotten, for when the coastal patrol scheme was resurrected in 1918 it was re-opened under the command of Flight Commander F.G. Andrea. Four canvas Bessoneaux hangars, a mess, an office and two cookhouses were quickly erected and Nos 517 and 518 (Special Duty) Flights were formed, and had reached full strength by the end of May 1918. Both Flights were equipped with the DH 6, an aircraft with only one merit—that of availability. They were joined in June by No 492 (Light Bomber) Flight operating the more effective DH 9.

After several changes of plan the unit at Prawle Point became No 254 Squadron, RAF, operating as part of No 72 Wing, No 9 Group, under the control of the Commander-in-Chief, Devonport. The Flights retained their separate identity and spent the rest of the war in fruitless and extremely boring patrols off south Devon. Eleven Armstrong huts, an Officers' Mess and a pigeon loft were under construction at the time of the Armistice but were not completed, the 180 men on strength remaining in tents or local billets.

With the Armistice flying all but ceased, No 254 Squadron being disbanded on February 22 1919. But the base remained open and by August 1919 was occupied by the Artillery Co-operation Squadron which used Sopwith 1½-Strutters amongst other types. This unit did not last long, however, and Prawle Point was closed in 1920, the land quickly reverting to agriculture.

Prestwick, Ayrshire (VII)

In 1945/46 the All Weather Flight of 24 Squadron was based here forming the Prestwick-London (Blackbushe)-Prestwick link with the BOAC Return Ferry Flight. Only two services were cancelled during the flight's year of existence.

Rattlesden, Suffolk (I)

Rattlesden served briefly as a site for Bloodhound defence missiles, in the hands of 257 Squadron. Prior to their arrival it was Wattisham's standby airfield.

Rattray (Crimond), Grampian (VII)

On February 8 1976 a Dove short of fuel on a flight from Stavanger to Aberdeen made a precautionary landing on the old perimeter track without damage. The name of this RNAS was changed from Crimond to Rattray on July 1 1945 in order to eliminate some confusion in postal addressing which had apparently caused official mail to go astray. The major part of the site was sold to a private

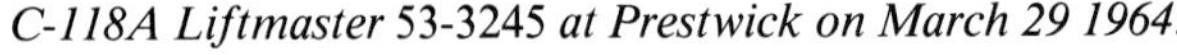

C-118A Liftmaster 53-3245 *at Prestwick on March 29 1964.*

Pulham Airship Station, on April 12 1926. The shed on the left was taken to Cardington where it remains. Huge screens shield the parking area by the airship sheds (via P.H.T. Green).

person in May 1963 but in 1973 484 of the 760 acres involved were bought back by the MoD for use as a wireless station.

Rednal, Shropshire (III)

A satellite was planned at Malpas but the Air Ministry Works Department turned the site down as unsuitable. An interesting dummy ops room remains on the former Instructional Site, identical to the building at Eshott in Northumberland. Other surviving structures include the decontamination centre, gymnasium and two Seagull Trenches, both of which have the machine-gun mountings still in place.

Renfrew, Strathclyde (VII)

The photograph on page 178 of Volume 7 is not of a Fokker F XXII but the Blackburn Civil Monoplane *G-ABKV* which flew from July 1934 as *K4241* with the A&AEE at Martlesham and was sold for scrap in April 1938. The author pleads gross carelessness in miscaptioning the photo!

Ridgewell, Essex (I)

An announcement in the summer of 1985 confirmed that MoD interest in this site remains, as indicated by a notice beside a 'T2' hangar here. Ridgewell is earmarked to be the site of an American wartime emergency hospital.

Ringway, Greater Manchester (III)

Extensive new development in the freight area centres around the two 'VR' hangars

A burning hut at Rendcombe after the crash on August 30 1917 of a 62 Squadron Bristol F 2B (P.H.T. Green collection and M. Hodgson).

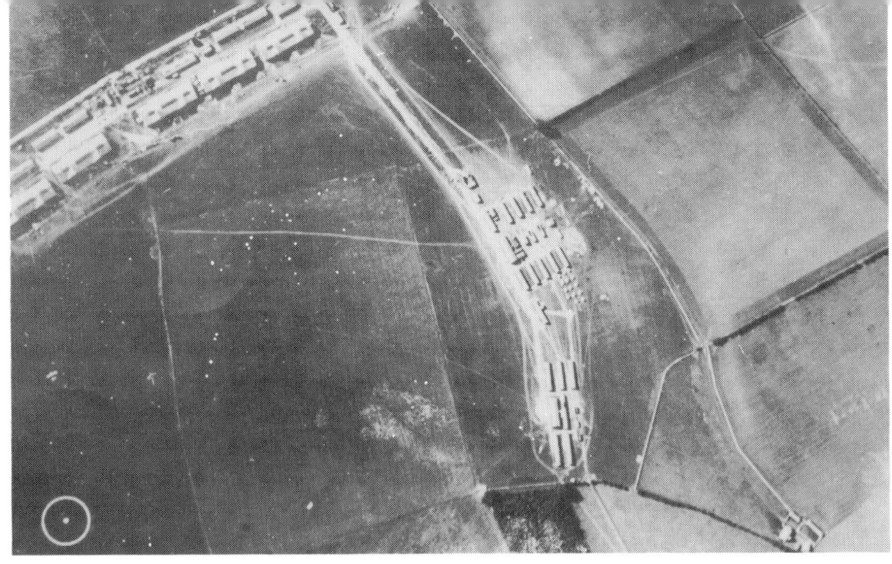

Aerial view of the 1914-1918 airfield at Rendcombe (P.H.T. Green collection and M. Hodgson).

of 1939 vintage. Another wartime survivor in this vicinity is the decontamination centre.

Roborough, Devon (V)

During 1984-85 Plymouth Airport (Roborough) underwent a £250,000 development programme aimed at reducing the number of weather diversions suffered by Brymon Airways. High intensity approach lighting was installed, and the navigational aids improved. The Roborough-Aberdeen scheduled service—the longest non-stop sector in the United Kingdom—is now well established and other developments include the setting up of an aircraft maintenance company on the airfield.

Rochford (Southend), Essex

See Southend.

Rollestone, Wiltshire (V)

Despite its exposed position on Salisbury Plain, the 180-acre site at Rollestone Camp proved ideal as a Balloon School, the small wood known as the Clump providing good shelter from the prevailing south-westerlies. By the Armistice in November 1918 the number of permanent staff giving advanced training on balloon operation and handling had reached 155 while the student population averaged 25 officers and 120 men. The technical site consisted of one canvas Bessoneau, three balloon beds (mooring sites), three store sheds and a gas producing plant.

The canvas erection mentioned in *Action Stations 5* was known as the 'Manby Screen' (see *Action Stations 2*) and was in position at Rollestone for a new series of trials by January 1940. The object was to enable the longest run to be

Manchester prototype at Ringway in 1938 (via Harry Holmes).

used on narrow landing grounds despite the prevailing wind. Trials at Rollestone were carried out using pilots and aircraft from CFS Upavon and it was quickly established that single-engined trainers could be operated safely in crosswinds up to 30 mph. The twin-engined Blenheim was a different matter, however, though it was considered that most of the problems were due to the badly ridged surface of the LG. Interest in the screen had largely evaporated by the end of 1940, but it was November 1941 before it was finally dismantled.

Following closure of the LG in July 1946, the camp was transferred to the Army who used the extensive domestic area as overflow accommodation for Larkhill, and for reservists training on the ranges. Thirty Nissen huts previously occupied by Territorials were surrounded by barbed wire and searchlights during the autumn of 1980 to accommodate part of the sudden increase in the prison population following riots that summer. Some 360 'low risk' prisoners were sent to Rollestone, looked after during the 1981 warders' pay dispute by soldiers from No 32 Guided Weapons Regiment. When the situation relaxed and the strain on prisons declined the camp was gradually closed, all prisoners having left Rollestone by the end of 1981.

Aeronautical links were reforged in the late 1970s when Short Brothers Air Services Ltd was formed at Rollestone to repair and service MATS-B target drones. Many of these drones were delivered to Rollestone for storage direct from Shorts' factories in Northern Ireland and were later prepared for use on ranges at Manobier, West Freugh, Otterburn, in the Hebrides, and at nearby Larkhill. Others were modified and/or rebuilt at the camp. In 1982 a number of MATS-B drones were sent to the Falklands to provide targets for the Rapier batteries which had been installed during and after the recapture of the islands.

Short Brothers lost the target drone operation contract to RCA in 1984 and the MATS-B drones still in storage were soon disposed of, the new company being only concerned with the Skeet target. It has recently (1987) been announced that Rollestone is again to become a prison—this time on a more permanent basis.

Ronaldsway, Isle of Man (III)

A dummy submarine conning tower was used as a target for the torpedo bombers. Early in 1942 the FAA were interested in a site at Mawbray in Cumberland which the RAF had decided not to proceed with. However, since it could not be completed until April 1944, the FAA decided to develop Ronaldsway instead.

St Angelo, Fermanagh (VII)

Allocated to the USAAF for an Air Support Command on February 28 1942 and then as a fighter CCRC on August 10 1942. The allocation was rescinded in April 1943 as surplus to 8th Air Force requirements and St Angelo was never occupied by the USAAF. An account of an incident at Christmas 1941 by Mr R.W.E. Humphreys conveys something of the flavour of life at these isolated aerodromes:

'On December 4 1941, six groundcrew (Fitter, Rigger, Electrician, Instrument Repairer and an Armourer (myself), three pilots and three Spitfires, went on detachment from 504 Squadron at Ballyhalbert to RAF St Angelo. At that time we were the only operational unit on the 'drome and we lived and ate in a log cabin near the shores of Loch Erne. Our only contact was with the driver of a truck who brought our food and mail. On December 25 we stood down from readiness as we had been invited to have dinner on the main camp.

'We turned up in our battered and greasy uniforms, the pilots in battle dress, to the astonishment of the well-groomed airmen and airwomen already seated. While our three pilots queued to bring us our grub, which was the traditional thing to do at this time of year, we found a spare table, waiting hopefully and aware of our status as "fighter types". However, a "bod" walked into the hall looking wildly around and collared the SWO who gestured in our direction. Our pilots shrieked out "Scramble" and we all tore out of the mess hall. Our previous van being immobilised (this was normal practice to defeat the Germans!) we comandeered another van and, with the driver accelerating up to 70 mph down slightly icy roads, we got back to our dispersal. We started all three Spitfires while the pilots struggled into their harnesses and into the cockpits. Then all three were away on to the only runway available (we were on one leg of the "L" shaped runways) and took off in formation. This was to intercept an unidentified aircraft approaching land.

'From the time of the "scramble"

signal in the mess to the time the three aircraft were airborne took nine minutes. I later heard that the AOC Northern Ireland had officially written a citation about this matter, but I never got mentioned in dispatches or heard that anyone else did.'

St Brides, South Glamorgan (III)

In November 1940 there were two separate sites known as St Brides East (No 5 SLG) and St Brides West (No 6 SLG). They were obviously adjacent as it was decided to combine them into one site as No 6 SLG on opening.

St Davids, Dyfed (III)

The Airwork Services aircraft were chiefly responsible for flying interception training missions for the Aircraft Direction Centre, HMS *Harrier*, at Kete. The Navy ceased using St Davids in 1958 and Airwork moved to Brawdy.

St Margarets (Dover), Kent

See Dover.

St Mary's, Scilly Isles (V)

The airport at St Mary's continues to lose money though the threat of closure, narrowly averted in 1983 by Government cash support, appears to have receded in recent years. British Airways have continued to provide a single S-61 helicopter for the Penzance-Scillies link and to operate the airfield through their subsidiary, International Aeradio Limited.

The Isle of Scilly Steamship Company, which has been operating the ferry 'Scillonian' for many years, started flying an Islander called the Skybus on light freight services between St Mary's and St Just in 1984. Three years later they finally got permission to fly passengers on the route, despite fierce opposition from councillors who feared loss of the helicopter service if more competition was approved than already provided by Brymon Airways.

St Mawgan, Cornwall (V)

No 236 (Nimrod) OCU returned from Kinloss during October 1983 with the Mk 2 version of the aircraft, and in 1984 No 42 Squadron completed conversion to this much improved anti-submarine 'hunter', now resplendent in hemp camouflage colours. The aircraft at St Mawgan are pooled, used as required by the squadron and the OCU.

An additional unit formed on November 1 1982. This was No 2625 (County of Cornwall) Squadron, Royal Auxiliary Air Force Regiment, a field squadron tasked with the ground defence of the airfield. Pitched against all the other auxiliary regiment units, No 2625 won the Strickland Cup in February 1985—a real feather in its cap.

The Officers' Mess has recently gained a second storey and a well-appointed accommodation annexe. The Sergeants' Mess has also been extended, while on the airfield the Fire Section has been completely rebuilt and various installations, including the control tower, have been 'toned down' with a coat of green paint.

Anti-submarine aircraft of other nations, notably US Navy, Norwegian and Dutch Orions, Canadian Auroras and Atlantics for the French and German navies are frequent visitors. A special effort is always made to have have as many of these aircraft as possible at open days, St Mawgan being the only RAF anti-submarine base in the country which regularly opens its gates to the public.

Brymon Airways continues to be the main user of the civil airport.

Samlesbury, Lancashire (III)

Lancashire Aircraft Corporation were doing Beaufighter repairs here in 1944. No 182 Gliding School formed here on May 28 1945 and remained until at least September 1949. No 635 GS moved here from Burtonwood in October 1983.

Sandy Bay (Lough Neagh), Antrim (VII)

The first Coronado service from New York arrived here on May 18 1944. Coronado *7223* was holed on some rocks on July 7 and was subsequently repaired on site.

Scampton, Lincolnshire (II)

Following the disbandment of Scampton's last V-Force squadron on March 31 1982, the station ceased to conduct flying operations pending its redevelopment as a unit with Royal Air Force Support Command. The station's reactivation started with the arrival of the Red Arrows who were deploying from Royal Air Force Kemble, Gloucestershire and became operational in April 1984. In September 1984 they were joined by Jet Provosts and Bulldogs

A typical display of disciplined formation flying by the Red Arrows.

of the Central Flying School which moved to Scampton from Royal Air Force Leeming in Yorkshire. The Headquarters Central Flying School also moved to Scampton.

The Red Arrows are a detachment of the Central Flying School (CFS), which is the oldest flight training establishment in the world, and comprise a team of nine pilots, a Manager and a Junior Engineering Officer. Away from base, the Red Arrows are supported by 27 travelling groundcrew, more usually referred to as 'front-line', while the Senior Engineering Officer and a further 50 technicians remain at Royal Air Force Scampton to service the aircraft on their return.

Aerobatics have always played a prominent part in Royal Air Force pilot training, and in the first Hendon pageant

Hunter FGA 9 (ex-79 Squadron) XG160, *one of the aircraft used by the Trade Management Training School at RAF Scampton.*

in 1920 there were performances by First World War biplanes. The CFS displayed with five Sopwith Snipes.

The arrival of fast, comparatively low-flying jets does not meet with an enthusiastic welcome from everyone. But the Red Arrows are something special and Lincolnshire is well used to the sight and sound of aircraft. From doom-laden heavy bombers during wartime, the Lincolnshire people now, in peacetime, have the world's top aerobatic team in their midst.

Two very nostalgic aircraft also moved with the School, those being the Vintage Pair, a de Havilland Vampire and a Gloster Meteor which are still flying thanks to the enthusiasm and dedication of the instructors at the RAF Central Flying School. They give up their free time to fly the aircraft which are now a part of aviation history and the Vintage Pair thrill thousands of people every year at air shows in the UK and abroad.

In February 1983 the Trade Management Training School for Junior NCOs formed at Scampton. The role of the School is to train NCOs in engineering management skills, for trade groups 1 and 2 (aircraft), and it has on strength a few single and two-seat Hunters. The first course started in April 1983. Another new unit to form was the Tornado Radar Unit which came into being at the end of 1983.

During the latter part of 1983 British Aerospace also moved to Royal Air Force Scampton from Holme-on-Spalding Moor in Yorkshire. The company have leased the land, the old Charlie Dispersal, on the far side of the airfield and have erected two mini-hangars. The British Aerospace unit became operational in the spring of 1984, and they fly in Phantoms and Buccaneers for Brough.

Sealand, Clwyd (III)

No 24 EFTS left in March 1946. Late in 1942, the Royal Navy investigated the possibility of basing an observer school here but nothing came of the proposal.

Seighford, Staffordshire (III)

No 21 PAFU ceased flying from here in May 1946.

Shobdon, Hereford and Worcester (III)

Mr W.K. Gilliland was an AC2 here in 1943/44 on the tow-rope Drop Zone and has written as follows: 'The incident of the B-17 landing took place in the early hours of the morning, the noise of the screaming brakes as the pilot tried to stop

Could you, at a glance, identify these as Douglas B-66s of the '47th' and based at Sculthorpe? Photographed in September 1964, and plentiful at that time.

Top *Hawker Furies of 5 FTS at Sealand in 1937* (J.W.G. Wellham via Chris Ashworth).

Above *Hart Trainers* K4918 *and* K4937 *of 5FTS, Sealand, in 1937* (J.W.G. Wellham via Chris Ashworth).

the 'plane overshooting woke everybody up.

'An incident you failed to mention in your book was the USAAF Dakota that "fell" out of the sky from about 300 ft in brilliant weather at 5 pm. We had just finished flying for the day when he pancaked on to the grass just beyond the control tower, smashing his port undercarriage, wing and engine. He was loaded with medical supplies for the US Army Hospital at Barrons Cross, near Leominster, and took off three days later after repair.'

Silloth, Cumbria (III)

One of the airfields considered in July 1944 for development as a national establishment for aeronautical research. It was said that there was sufficient room to build a runway up to 8,000 yd in length.

Skeabrae, Orkney (VII)

No 1476 Advanced Ship Recognition Flight disbanded here on January 1 1944. No 232 Squadron moved in on October 13 1940.

Skellingthorpe, Lincolnshire (II)

Very little remains of the old wartime airfield which has now been overrun by a housing estate. A new school has been built on part of the old airfield, appropriately named the Manser School, Birchwood, Lincoln. Flying Officer Leslie Manser was awarded the Victoria Cross posthumously for actions which saved his crew during a bombing raid on Cologne, in May 1942. The school was opened by Flying Officer Manser's brother Cyril in April 1981.

Sleap, Shropshire (III)

Official closure date was to be December 26 but a Christmas party lasted longer than intended! No 34 MU was present from July 1947 until moving to Stoke Heath (Tern Hill) circa 1949.

Gladiators from 607 Squadron, Usworth, over Seaburn in 1939 (via J. Relph).

Snailwell, Cambridgeshire (I)

Page 31 of *Action Stations 1* carried a photograph of one of the few East Anglian Blister hangars remaining in their original positions. No more, for in 1982 Snailwell's almost last physical feature was quickly felled.

Reference to the Belgian Training School deserves expansion. One element undertook technical training using in 1946 three Lancasters, a Halifax VI, a Beaufighter VI and a Tempest V. The other gave flying training using Tiger Moths and Master IIs. Early in 1945 Westley (which in 1945-46 was used by the ATC for Kirby Cadet glider flying) acted as satellite station, but Bottisham was later used instead because of its better facilities.

Snailwell was a grass airfield with three prescribed runways, ENE/WSW of 1,680 yd, NNE/SSW of 1,430 yd and ESE/WNW of 1,420 yd. It had one Bellman and ten Blister hangars by late 1944, a dozen twin-engine type hardstandings and two frying-pan type.

Southend, (Rochford) Essex (VIII and IX)

Southend Airport could become a very profitable stopping off point for many short-haul feeder lines and the aircraft most suitable is the BAe 146 airliner. Southend has an efficient rail link to the centre of London.

On March 1 1985 the Southend Municipal Council handed over management of the airport to British Airports International, a subsidiary of the British Airports Authority, and International Aeradio Ltd. The company already manages Exeter and Southampton airports for both these city councils and hopes to turn the yearly £500,000 loss at Southend into a profit within three years.

Over the years Southend Airport has seen a decline in business as a result of runway restrictions but changes are in the wind and in May 1985 the closure of runway 15/33 was being considered in order to release more land for more valuable purposes.

At May 1985 Southend Airport housed five flying clubs—the Southend Flying club, Eastern Counties Aero Club, Thames Estuary Flying Club, Seawing Flying Club and Skylane Flight Centre. Their aircraft are a mixed bag of twin-engined Beeches, Cessnas, etc, and in total there are some 70 club and private light aircraft based at the airfield.

Helicopter Hire operate out of Southend Airport with a fleet of seven helicopters for charter work. Harvest Air is also resident here and operates on behalf of the Department of Trade, spraying oil slicks from the air.

Southend Airport can boast the most advanced radar control system in the world. It is the S.511 airfield surveillance radar designed by Marconi Radar at Chelmsford and it is sited on the north apron on permanent loan. Marconi selected Southend Airport to demonstrate the radar system and they invite potential customers from all over the world to come and see the radar system in operation.

Speke, Merseyside (III)

On September 6 1942 Seafire *AD371* made the type's first rocket launch during a trial on the Speke catapult. It was planned to replace MSFU's Hurricanes with Seafires but this did not in fact occur.

The pre-war terminal closed in April 1986 when the new terminal on the southern airfield was completed. Thereafter the north airfield has been progressively withdrawn from use but aircraft are still hangared there. Still visible on the corner of Hangar No 1 is the inscription 'CAUTION B-24 AIRCRAFT'. This is strange because Liberators were not among the aircraft types handled by the Lockheed facility at Speke. The Bellman hangar once used by the FAA was dismantled in 1984.

Squires Gate, Lancashire (III)

Add 42 E&RFTS spring 1939 to September 3 1939 (Tiger Moth) and 9 CANS September 25 1939 to May 27 1940 (Anson). The School of Air-Sea Rescue was based in Blackpool town but had a Flight of Ansons here from March 1943 to February 1945. Squires Gate was one of the airfields considered in July 1944 for development as a national establishment for aeronautical research with a runway extension up to 5,000 yd.

Stansted, Essex (officially now London/Stansted) (I)

TL372229.

Yet again—the Stansted Aviation Opera. Stansted is to become London's third airport, and major changes are likely to have begun in 1986. There is no question about it, the airfield and its 10,000-ft runway 05/23 (PCN 86) has long been underutilised and expansion seems largely intended to ensure maximum use of existing Stansted, which entails sweeping changes since the airfield's rail and road links are poor. Finding sufficient personnel to staff any enlargement of Stansted will also need careful planning.

One thing is beyond question, Stansted witnessed one of the most astonishing aeronautical sights ever seen in East Anglia when in June 1983 a modified Boeing 747 brought, on its back, an

One of the most amazing aviation bonanzas of recent years was the visit to Stansted of the Space Shuttle Enterprise, *a non-orbital vehicle.*

Temporary canvas hangars set up in the north-east corner of Stonehenge aerodrome photographed on March 22 1918. A couple of 0/100s can be seen amongst the numerous single-engined bombers in use for training (E.F. Cheesman).

example of the American Space Shuttle. Just how many viewers flocked to the Stansted area over the three days involved is uncertain, but an amazing two million seems a low estimate.

Stansted has continued to be used for short-range flights to the Continent, special and charter flights, business flights, post office night flights and freight runs by Belfasts and the CL-44 'Guppy' of Heavy Lift. Mainly it is the Fokker F 27s of AirUK and Short SD3-30s of Jersey European Airways and Air Ecosse which are regularly seen here, although an assortment of others call. It remains disappointing to see how low has been Stansted's utilisation ever since it became a civilian airport. After the B-26s left Stansted, with its 56 circular hardstandings and three 2,000-yd runways, it became a USSTAF Air Depot. In the immediate post-war period it was Bassingbourn's listed satellite and still known as Stansted Mountfitchet. As Stansted it soon became North Weald's standby where in wartime that station's RAuxAF Vampires would have been accommodated.

Stonehenge, Wiltshire

SU114421. 3½ miles W of Amesbury, straddling the A303(T)

Stranded in the middle of a modern road complex, the mysterious ring of granite pillars making up Stonehenge look rather

The main technical site at Stonehenge in September 1918. The hangars are in the southern corner of the aerodrome with Normanton Down in the middle distance and Lake Down hangars on the skyline (E.F. Cheesman).

A closer view of the main Stonehenge technical site in September 1918 when No 1 School of Navigation and Bomb Dropping was fully established with numerous de Havilland and Handley Page bombers on strength. Despite the many wooden huts to the rear of the hangars, tents are still in wide-scale use (P.Liddle via G.S. Leslie).

lost these days. In 1917 they must have been much more impressive, and doubtless became etched on the memories of many a young airman flying from the large aerodrome built just to the west of the prehistoric site.

Work on the training aerodrome of Stonehenge started early in 1917. It emerged as an almost rectangular 360-acre aerodrome bounded to the north by the present A360 road from Amesbury to Shrewton, and to the east by the minor road from Durrington to Normanton Downs. It was built to house two training units but No 108 Squadron, an embryo operational unit, was the first occupant when it formed on November 11 1917. It was joined on December 2 by No 2 TDS from nearby Lake Down, but this day-bomber training unit had hardly settled in before it was re-designated No 1 School of Navigation & Bomb Dropping on January 5 1918.

No 1 SofN&BD was intended as a finishing school for pilots and observers. It was divided into two squadrons, one for airmen destined for day bombers, the other for those going on to night bombers, principally the twin-engined Handley Page 0/400. To provide training on the latter the Naval Handley Page School moved in from Manston during January to join the DH 4s, DH 9s and FE 2Bs of the SofN&BD. Hangarage was first provided by a line of canvas Bessoneaux, while personnel were accommodated in

A Handley Page 0/100 of the School of Navigation and Bomb Dropping at Stonehenge (E.F. Cheesman).

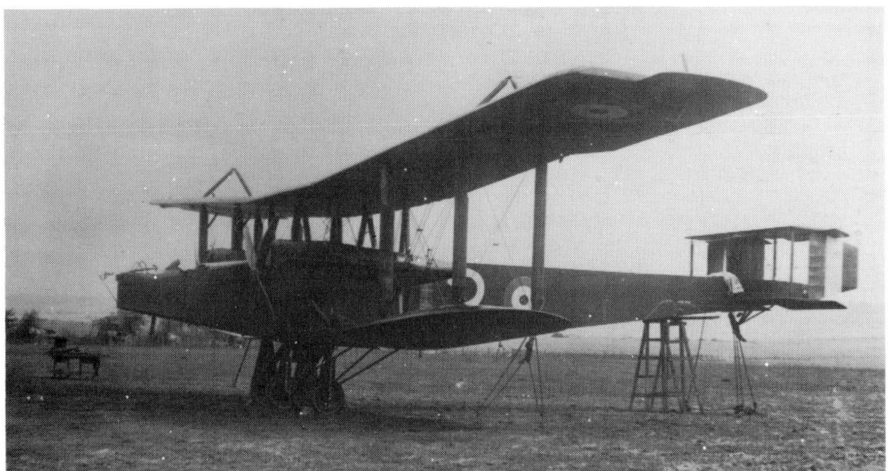

Two ladies having their photograph taken with a highly coloured Sopwith Snipe in one of the GS hangars at Stonehenge—shortly after the end of the war (via T. Hancock).

tents, but by early 1918 work was well advanced on eight GS aeroplane sheds (built in pairs), a repair shed and numerous workshops. Construction of four semi-permanent Handley Page sheds had also started on a separate site.

The day bomber pilots and observers were given instruction in navigation, cloud flying, formation flying, gunnery and map-reading while aspiring night flyers practised day/night navigation by map reading and compass flying, bombing, and the use of the vertical searchlight. The monthly output of the school gradually increased to 60 day and 60 night crews, using two Avro 504Ks and six Maurice Farmans for initial checks, 48 DH 4/DH 9s for day bomber training, and 40 FE 2B pusher biplanes and ten 0/400 twin-engined bombers at night. The night trainees had great difficulty getting adequate rest during the day so a separate hutted camp was authorized well away from the aerodrome. It was the only part of the station not complete at the end of the war.

Training continued, albeit at a reduced rate, until July 1919 when the school moved temporarily to Old Sarum before amalgamation with No 2 SofN&BD at Andover on September 23 1919. It was replaced at Stonehenge by the Artillery Co-operation School in August, but flying from the aerodrome was severely restricted during the autumn and any aerial demonstrations required were provided by 'art obs' aircraft operating from Worthy Down.

At the end of March 1920 the Artillery Co-op School was absorbed by the School of Army Co-operation (the renamed RAF/Army Co-operation School), Worthy Down, but continued to operate from Stonehenge. 'C' Flight of No 4 Squadron moved in from Farnborough during April 1920, its Bristol F 2Bs providing artillery spotting, recce and photographic demonstration as well as bombing and ground strafing experience for troops of the Aldershot Command on Salisbury Plain. The 'Brisfits' remained until October when 'C' Flight transferred to Old Sarum with the whole of the SofAC.

Stonehenge was then closed and some buildings were auctioned while others were used for a time by the nearby Pedigree Stock Farm. The sites were gradually cleared during the 1920s, among the last substantial items to go being the multi-bay Handley Page sheds near Fargo Plantation. They were finally dismantled early in the 1930s, parts being re-erected at High Post, Old Warden and Woodley (where they formed part of the Phillip & Powis/Miles Aircraft factory complex).

After 65 years there is now very little evidence of this important First World War aerodrome on the original site. It is, however, surprising that such a large and busy station in such a prominent position could disappear so completely from the public's memory—but then Stonehenge is a mysterious place.

Stormy Down, South Glamorgan (III)

No 68 Gliding School formed by December 1944 at Bridgend and moved to Stormy Down early in 1945. To St Athan March 1947. The hangars are 'F' types *not* 'VR's.

Stornoway, Western Isles (VII)

The Vampires which made the first east-west Atlantic crossing by jet aircraft in July 1948 were from 54 Squadron. On July 19 1948, 16 Shooting Stars of the 56th Fighter Group staged through Stornoway having made the first west-east jet crossing en route to Germany.

Stretton, Cheshire (III)

The ATC Gliding School was No 187. Operations were suspended in November 1947. The airfield closed on November 4 1958. The Air Yard with its Pentad hangars is now an industrial estate, as is most of the former technical area. The tower still stands near the M56 motorway and at least one fighter pen survives on the southern perimeter.

Strubby, Lincolnshire (II)

On July 1 1944 No 404 Squadron Royal Canadian Air Force moved from No 19 Group, Davidstow Moor, to No 16 Group—No 154 (General Reconnaissance) Wing, at Strubby. Their stay was for only a few weeks and on September 2 1944 they moved to No 18 Group at Banff in Scotland.

The heliport at Strubby is still operational and Bond Helicopters use the airfield as its main base. They operate a fleet of French helicopters and do the servicing for BP in the North Sea.

Sullom Voe, Shetland (VII)

The hulk of the Catalina in which Flying Officer (later Lieutenant) John Cruickshank won the VC is said to be still lying where it was run aground.

Sumburgh, Shetland (VII)

A few wartime buildings still exist, including the decontamination centre and squash court.

Swannington, Norfolk (I)

The extent of the airfield's survival was clear from comment in Volume 1. The reason was that in 1951 it was earmarked for complete expansion to accommodate two SRD fighter squadrons and an all-weather squadron to be brought in from Horsham St Faith. Rehabilitation came close, but few such stations eventually re-

Attacker WK326 *of 1831 Squadron on approach to Stretton, circa 1955* (via S.G. Jones).

opened. One was Shepherd's Grove (originally called Hepworth), another Bentwaters, each of which was fitted out sufficiently to accommodate a squadron of US fighters brought in under Operation 'Galloper' during 1951, along with Wethersfield which was also developed initially for only one US squadron.

Sway, Hampshire

SZ287981. See text for directions.

One of the first letters received after the publication of *Action Stations 5* was from Mr Ralph H. Dargue of New Milton, Hampshire, whose interest had been aroused by a one-line mention of Sway ELG in the section on Christchurch airfield, and he wanted to know more. I could add little, and the ELG's precise location was unknown for no official list of these sites has yet come to light in the Public Record Office or elsewhere.

Undeterred, Ralph Dargue set to work and within six months presented me with a remarkably detailed dossier on Sway ELG and an account of how he had gone about his investigation. He gave permission for this work to be published and it is presented here, only slightly edited, as an example of what can still be discovered about an obscure landing ground 40 years after its closure by a bit of intelligent deduction and 'on the spot' enquiries.

The first steps

'Enquiry at the PRO, the Local Authority Planning Department, the Forestry Commission and an interview with a local historian failed to produce any insight as to where the airfield (ELG) had actually been sited. Thus an investigation using large scale OS maps had to be undertaken to identify areas large enough for even single-seat aircraft to land and take-off. Enough space between two contours was the first hint of a possibility, and it is surprising how few such areas exist within a couple of miles of any named village (in Dorset/Hampshire anyway). Modern agriculture has shown a preference for the barbed wire fence whereas in the past hedgerows or trees were used for demarcation and shelter —perhaps for a century or more. Their removal is another useful sign.

'The absence of ruined Maycrete buildings, hardstandings, hangars or pill boxes on ELGs make things more difficult, and one has to rely very much on the inspired hunch. Having selected suitable places the next step is to ask around the locality and even though there may have been an almost total turn-over in population during the intervening years, there is usually an 'oldest inhabitant' whose memory may be tapped. In the case of Sway, the land between Pitmore Lane and Coombe Lane looked most promising, and a polite call at a couple of the older cottages on the edge of the Forest was the first exploratory step in this direction. The enquiries led to the village store whose owner directed one's steps towards the village baker—and here indeed was good fortune. The present baker had seen the 'occupation' before he had himself put on RAF uniform, and a couple of airmen had been billeted on his parents. The airfield location could now be definitely identified as that of Manor Farm, where the farmer and his wife had been in occupation when the land was explored and commandeered by the investigating officer from Christchurch.

'Once these basic details had been passed to the local historian other sources

Panoramic view across Sway ELG taken from the eastern boundary (R.H. Dargue).

Sway Tower (280967) Paul's Place (287976) Little Combe (28697

were soon found, and in this case correspondence and phone calls produced more detail from a former airman attached to Sway ELG, and another contact who had witnessed most of the activities around Sway during the war years. His memories of the period July 1940 to late 1941 were usefully tapped and slowly the following story emerged.

The airfield

'The landing ground of about 106 acres was created by grubbing out hedgerows, filling hollows and planing off the hump in the middle of fields known as Park, Coombe, 12-acre, 14-acre, 7-acre and 16-acre, all part of Manor Farm (OS Ref SZ287981) between Pitmore Lane and Coombe Lane, Sway. The northern edge of the area was the back of properties facing on to Chapel Lane. The levelling work was carried out by Irish labourers who arrived in the village "out of the blue" asking people, "Where was the airfield?". With thoughts of invasion uppermost in people's minds they were taken to be Germans in disguise until their identities were established.

'The longest landing and take-off run was on bearing 130/310 but there were lateral obstructions; an elm tree at SZ288981 and a hedge which extended to SZ291982. Between Manor Farm and Birchy Hill is the Sway Coombe with a stream bed level 75 ft above sea level, while the farm itself stands at 128 ft and the top of Sway Tower (Peterson's Folly) at GR280967 reaches 315 ft some ¾ mile from the centre of the ELG. This tower was an excellent point of reference for enemy pilots flying on a direct line from the Needles Lighthouse to Middle Wallop or Swindon, with Southampton just to the east of the flight line.

'No buildings were erected on the LG, activity being conducted from tents in the NW corner near Little Purley Farm, by Horseshoe Cottage and by Little Acre on Pauls Lane. The wind direction was given to pilots by mounting strips of canvas on a long pole, no proper windsock being erected.

Airfield activities

August-September 1940

'A Special Duty Unit had been formed at Martlesham Heath early in 1940 and its Harrows were moved to Christchurch during May. 'X' Flight was detached to the Sway ELG early in August with six men (1 GD Corporal, 1 LAC Fitter, two Flight Riggers, two Armourers) to tend the aircraft used for radar evaluation and development. About ten aircraft, including at least one Battle, were sent to the site, an Anson being used to ferry men and equipment to and from the LG. Only two Blenheims and the Battle were actually used on the trials—and then infrequently.

'The Flight was commanded by Flight Lieutenant Burke—who was apparently stationed at Christchurch. In September the complement rose to about 18 men with a Sergeant in charge at Sway, all billeted in the village. One family took in six and the baker housed another two, the airmen using a path alongside Purley Cottage as a short cut to the ELG. The owner of the cottage built a substantial shelter by digging into the boundary bank and covering the hole with heavy timbers topped by galvanised iron sheets and a thick layer of earth and sods. Bombs fell nearby one night and the whole family had just taken cover when several airmen rushed in declaring that it was too 'hot' for them outside. Grandma was most upset by this intrusion, especially when she counted heads and found they numbered 13!

Manor Farm (287981) North Sway Cottage (286982)

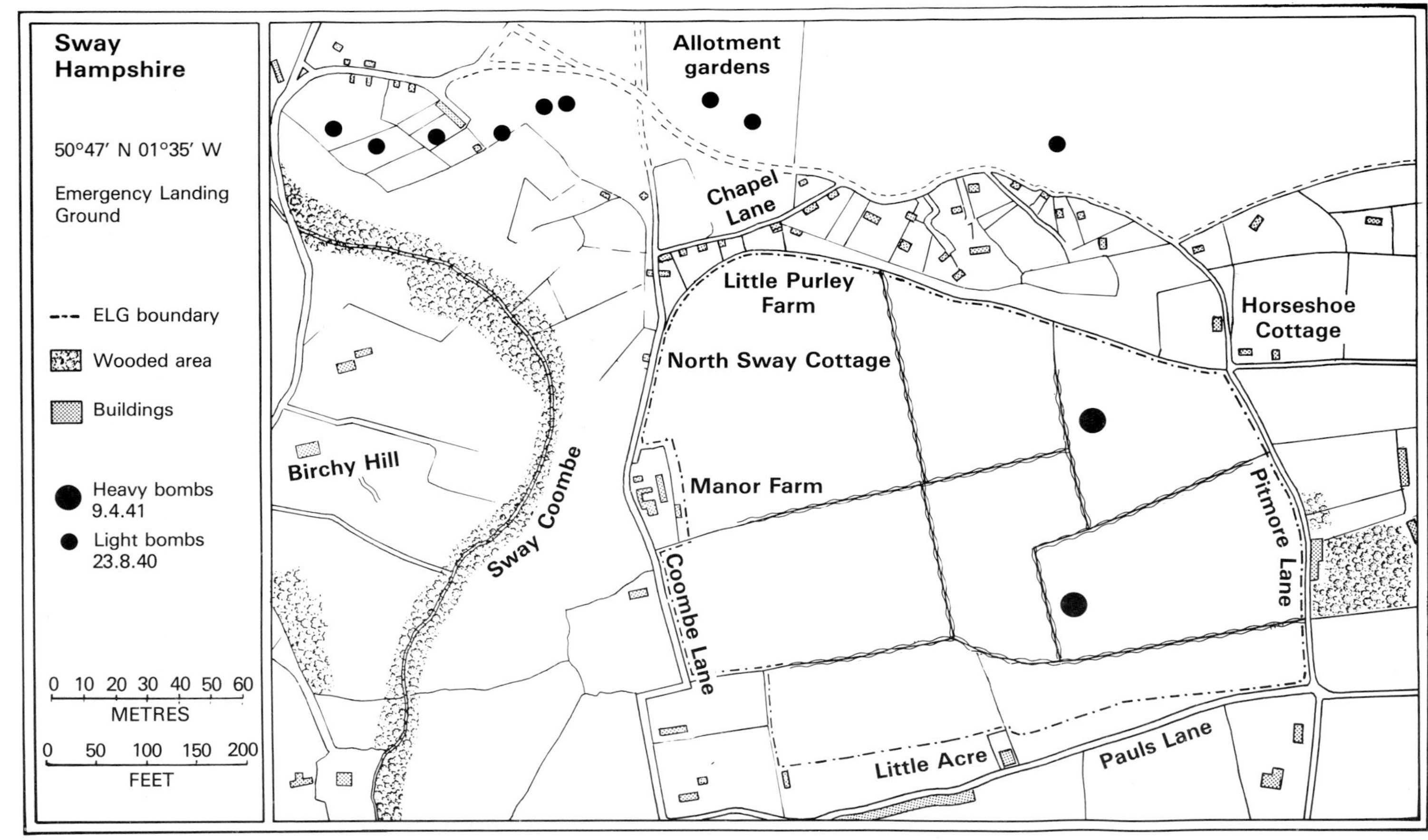
Sway
Hampshire
50°47′ N 01°35′ W
Emergency Landing Ground
ELG boundary
Wooded area
Buildings
Heavy bombs 9.4.41
Light bombs 23.8.40
0 10 20 30 40 50 60
METRES
0 50 100 150 200
FEET
Allotment gardens
Chapel Lane
Little Purley Farm
North Sway Cottage
Horseshoe Cottage
Birchy Hill
Manor Farm
Sway Coombe
Coombe Lane
Pitmore Lane
Little Acre
Pauls Lane

October 1940-October 1941

'In October 1940 the unit and some of its Harrows were transferred to Middle Wallop, but other aircraft replaced them and were parked as before along the northern perimeter between North Sway Cottage on Coombe lane and Horseshoe Cottage on Pitmore Lane. The Anson was usually parked in the 16-acre field until the raid which damaged another aircraft (said to be a Hampden). It was then moved to the 'tail' of the 7-acre, behind 'Little Acre' in Pauls Lane, by a Fitter who turned out to have insufficient experience on soft ground. The airmen holding the wingtips were almost dragged off their feet when he opened the throttles too much and the aircraft careered at high speed towards the rear of Manor Farm, only stopping when the undercarriage became embedded in a bank of earth.

'The aircraft were often deployed back to Christchurch to aid the decoy nature of the ELG and for trial modifications, the only other general activity being routine servicing and engine running. It would seem that the airmen were also engaged in 'flogging' aviation fuel to the villagers! In the early days there were also several landings by fighters (usually Hurricanes) at Sway, their pilots seeking directions to their home bases. In the autumn of 1940 a damaged Hurricane force-landed to the east of the allotment gardens, the pilot escaping with minor injuries. It was dismantled and taken away by road.

'The ELG was abandoned during the late autumn of 1941 after the aircraft had departed and the airmen dispersed.

Enemy action

'The Luftwaffe made a number of attacks on the ELG, about 100 bombs of varying calibre falling near Sway. The most memorable occasions were:

'August 23 1940—the day New Milton was 'blitzed' and a stick of ten bombs fell to the north of the ELG. One dropped down a well in front of a cottage on Back Lane, and another showered cottages on Chapel Lane with potatoes from the allotments.

'April 9 1941—two heavy bombs fell on the ELG at night. One exploded near the end of the hedgerow between the 12- and 14-acre fields damaging a Hampden, and the other erupted at the southern end of the 7- and 16-acre fields early the next morning. One of the cows took fright and was eventually found on the far side of the 16-acre with two aircraft guards who were still hiding under the hedge.

Present day

'Barbed wire fences mark where hedgerows stood before the site was commandeered in July 1940, and cattle graze contentedly. The elm tree has been felled after succumbing to disease.'

Acknowledgements: the credit for putting this story together goes to Ralph Dargue but much of the information came from Mrs Brain (Manor Farm); Mr Jack Parker (village baker); Mr Eric Pardey, who as a boy lived at Purley Cottage, and Mr Roy Taylor, an erstwhile member of 'X' Flight, SDF.

Swinderby, Lincolnshire (II)

In 1979 the Flying Selection Squadron (FSS) formed at Swinderby. The FSS is equipped with Chipmunks, which are most suitable for the role of the FSS which provides a means of filtering out potential failures in the pilot training

Sway Tower and electricity lines dominated the south-western side of the ELG—especially at take-off (R.H. Dargue).

intake before they reach the expensive jet stages of training. At present only students with less than about 30 hours of previous flying training go through flying selection, but having graduated from FSS a student transfers to jets secure in the knowledge that he has a realistic chance of success.

In September 1982 the Women's Royal Air Force training moved to Swinderby from Hereford and the first recruits arrived the following month to join non-commissioned airmen at Swinderby School of Recruit Training. It is the first time in Royal Air Force history that basic training for men and women has been on the same base. As officers are trained at Royal Air Force Cranwell it now means that every recruit will begin his or her RAF life in Lincolnshire.

The manning plan for 1985 called for some 5,500 RAF and 600 WRAF recruits which means that at any one time Swinderby's staff are coping with a transient population of up to 1,200 recruits. To meet this task Swinderby has a permanent staff of around 400, including 45 civilians.

The station is organised into two wings—Admin and Training. The latter embodies Recruit Training Squadrons supported by instructors from the Royal Air Force Regiment and Physical Education Squadron. Each squadron has six flights of Royal Air Force recruits and one flight of WRAF girls.

The station badge consists of the torch of learning against a portcullis in the background. Its motto, *Haec Porta, Moenia Viri*, means 'Here are the gates, the men are the walls'.

Sydenham (Belfast Harbour), Down (VII)

Has now been re-named Belfast Harbour to reflect its advantage in being nearer to the city than Aldergrove. Used extensively by Manx Airlines for scheduled services since Shorts decided to exploit it as a civil airport.

Syerston, Nottinghamshire (II)

Royal Air Force Newton took over parenting responsibilities for Syerston in 1970 and much of Syerston is now disused. The airfield has good runways and buildings and it is difficult to understand why Newton, with only grass runways, does not move into Syerston. However, the airfield continues to fulfil a valuable role with gliding for the Air Cadets Central Gliding School and Royal Air Force police dog training also taking place here. Syerston is now one of the few remaining wartime airfields with many of its original buildings still standing.

Tatenhill, Staffordshire (III)

The correct date for the Fauld bomb store explosion was November *27* 1944.

Tatton Park, Cheshire (III)

There is a memorial here to the Parachute Training School.

Teddesley Park, Staffordshire (III)

The actual location of this SLG is further to the north at SJ960155 where a Robin hangar still exists. A Pawnee used the site in 1964 for crop spraying.

Templeton, Dyfed (III)

The USAAF 1st Gunnery & Tow Target Flight was present here from December 14 1943 to May 8 1944 with Lysanders and Masters, and No 74 Gliding School 1945/46. Templeton is now a local council

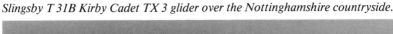

Slingsby T 31B Kirby Cadet TX 3 glider over the Nottinghamshire countryside.

Sector Operations block at Tern Hill, a surface building with traversed walls all around it.

commercial vehicle testing ground. Built across two hills, one runway has a very deep dip in the middle. Used today by private aircraft.

Tern Hill, Shropshire (III)

Although official records state that the German raider on October 16 1940 was a Do 17, John Didsbury disagrees and writes as follows:

'The aircraft which made the one and only raid on Tern Hill was certainly not a Dornier, but a Ju 88. My authority for this statement is that around 7.30 on the morning of that date I glanced up to see what, in the early morning mist, I thought was a 29 Squadron Blenheim about to "shoot up" after a night patrol. This they had done on a few occasions previously. I was puzzled by the appearance as the machine approached head-on to me and then noticed the bomb doors open.

'Four bombs (probably 250 kgs) flew over my head at around 300 ft and I clearly remember the bomb-aimer's face with his goggles pushed up on his forehead. By the time they exploded, I was diving under my bed in one of 24 MU's billets at the end of the hangar line. I afterwards found the bombs had fallen in open space behind the control tower (blowing over the wooden bombing trainer tower) and later learned that incendiaries were responsible for the hangar fire which you mention. No mine was dropped, only two thuds as the two pairs of bombs hit in succession.

'No Spitfires of 611's Flight, dispersed in what we used to call the "fighter corner" (by No 3, or "B" site, at the crossroads) took off at all, but after a short while two Spitfires from an unknown unit flew low eastwards over Stoke Heath.'

The station is now an Army camp but gliding still takes place.

Teversham (Cambridge), Cambridgeshire

See Cambridge.

Thorpe Abbotts, Suffolk (I)

Little remains of the three concrete and wood chip-coated runways (099 of 2,100 yd, 043 and 350 of 1,400 yd in length). There were two 'T2' hangars here, and 50 concrete hardstandings. At Thorpe Abbotts may now be found in the one-time control tower a fine privately established museum recalling wartime days and the stay here of the 100th Bomb Group, the 'Bloody Hundredth' which suffered such heavy losses. Well worth a visit.

Tilstock (Whitchurch Heath), Shropshire (III)

Most of the buildings on the former technical site by the A41 have now been demolished. A Spanish-built Junkers 52 on its way to an air display force-landed here with low oil pressure in May 1985.

Tiree, Strathclyde (VII)

The floors of the former hangars are still dotted around the perimeter.

Toller, Dorset

SY540980. 10 miles ENE of Bridport off minor roads.

A sub-station for the Mullion airship base

was constructed at Toller during the spring of 1918 and commissioned in No 9 Group, Plymouth, later in the year. Located 1½ miles west of Toller Porcorum in woodland immediately north-west of Gray's Farm, and well protected from the prevailing winds, it was usually occupied by a SS Zero non-rigid on detachment from Mullion. *SSZ27* was *in situ* at the end of the war, this airship being deflated at Toller on December 3 1918. The sub-station was de-activated later in the month, and abandoned early in 1919.

A Short 184 of 418 Flight being lifted out of the water at RNAS Torquay by the pier crane (P. Liddle via G.S. Leslie).

Toome, Londonderry (VII)

Tentatively allocated to the USAAF for an Air Support Command February 28 1942 and then to the 8th Air Force as a bomber training base on August 10 1942. Officially transferred to the USAAF on July 26 1942, and returned to the RAF on November 7 1944. A detachment of 203 Gliding School flew from here in the early 1950s.

Torquay, Devon

SX919632. Close to town centre off A379 road.

The opening of RNAS Torquay early in 1918 completed the chain of flying boat, airship and floatplane bases which stretched out to the Scillies and enabled continuous cover to be provided for convoys in the south-west approaches. Nestling inside the harbour on four acres of ground between the South and Haldon Piers, the site proved to be one of the most sheltered of the many seaplane bases scattered around the coast of Britain, though entering and leaving the harbour through the narrow gap in the breakwater could be hazardous.

To house the established 12 Short 184 floatplanes, four small seaplane sheds were erected alongside three Bessoneaux canvas hangars, but the site was dominated by a balloon shed used by a detachment from No 16 Balloon Base, Merifield, which operated a sub-station at Torquay. Crew rooms and technical stores were also provided on the site but all domestic accommodation was requisitioned in the town, the 'Sea Haven Hotel' being taken over, while No 11 Beacon Terrace became the Women's hostel and the coastguard boat house their rest room.

The base had a water frontage of 450 ft and, although a slipway was constructed, a crane was usually used to lower the floatplanes on to the water. Space was a problem from the start and in the event only six Short 184s could be based, these being taken over by No 418 Flight during June 1918 when the original plan envisaging the operation of a second Flight, No 419, was abandoned. Despite this, No 239 Squadron, RAF, was formed in August and operated No 418 Flight under the control of No 72 Wing, No 4 (Operations) Group. The unit flew largely uneventful patrols for the rest of the war, the squadron finally disbanding on May 15 1919. RAF Torquay was relinquished in August 1919, the site being handed over to

RNAS Tresco, Scilly Isles, with the main steel-framed seaplane sheds under construction. The slipway and a beached H 12 flying boat are clearly visible (P. Liddle via G.S. Leslie).

the Government Surplus Property Board.

'Joyriding' Avro floatplanes used the slipway and the site for a year or two during the early 1920s but the public's appetite for flying soon faded, and the marine operators (who had to charge more than the five shillings (25p) almost universal amongst landplane 'barnstormers') were the first to close down.

During World War 2 the high-speed launches of No 39 Air-Sea Rescue unit were based at Torquay but no sign of the site remains except the slipway close to the Redcliffe Hotel.

Tresco, Scilly Isles

SV890149. ½ mile S of New Grimsby, Tresco.

A visit to the garden isle of Tresco is an essential part of any holiday on the Scilly Isles, made easier since April 1983 by the introduction of a helicopter link. The time-honoured boat crossing from St Mary's can be very rough and few would imagine it to be an ideal location for a flying boat base — but it was to prove a very successful one between 1917 and 1919!

Operation of Short 184 floatplanes from moorings in the Scillies had been tried unsuccessfully during 1916 but, following another horrific bout of merchant ship sinkings late that same year, the Admiralty decided to try again. This time flying boats were to be employed and an urgent investigation of possible sites on St Mary's was undertaken during January 1917. The Porth Mellon (SV908107) area, just to the east of the lifeboat station, was chosen and on February 26 the first of three Curtiss H 12 'Large America' boats arrived, followed by the others two days later. One of these, serialled *8656,* had picked up two 65-lb bombs at Newhaven and did an anti-submarine patrol en route — this counting as the first operational sortie of the detachment.

Under the command of Squadron Leader R. Hope-Vere the flying boats started using the 'Spider's Web' patrol plan evolved at Great Yarmouth, supplemented by a number of Short 184s which had arrived in crates. It was soon obvious that the extended air cover was effective but Porth Mellon was too exposed, and after making a further survey of all the Scilly Isles, Flight Commander R. B. Maycock, RN, suggested a site on Tresco. His plan was approved and a roughly rectangular 20-acre piece of low-lying land near New Grimsby was requisitioned.

Bounded on the landward by Hacket Town Lane, the Great Pool and Pool

Many of the Tresco flying-boat base buildings are still in use, and the remains of the slipway can be seen in this photograph taken in May 1979 (R.W. Elliott).

Road, the site fronted the almost land-locked New Grimsby harbour, a strip of water 1½ miles long and ½ mile wide between Tresco and Bryher. Although the tide in the harbour was strong the water was usually calm and provided an excellent take-off and landing area as well as safe moorings for about six large flying boats.

Initially facilities were primitive, the Admiralty sanctioning nothing more than a large Bessoneau hangar, 200 ft × 120 ft, a rudimentary slipway and a few tents. Personnel were ferried across from St Mary's daily, but as RNAS Tresco showed its worth conditions on the island were slowly improved and during the early summer of 1917 a 'permanent' air station was authorised. Built by No 1 Air Construction Section, RNAS, it consisted of small hutted camps on dispersed sites near New Grimsby and workshops, flight offices and wooden hangars on the main base. The hangars were used while work continued on two large steel-framed seaplane sheds. A much improved slipway was also constructed, this carrying a two-ton capacity track-mounted trolley, easily capable of transporting flying boats from the hardstanding down into the water — and retrieving them for servicing. A small 'floating-dock' was later provided for work on the two Short 184s usually on the Tresco inventory.

Most patrols were uneventful but the faithful H 12, *8656,* was soon in action, the crew sighting a U-boat on May 27 1917. Two 100-lb bombs were observed to hit the submarine forward of the conning tower and it sank at a 60 degree angle, the stern coming right out of the water. Two days later another U-boat was attacked by *8656* with four 100-pounders, resulting in a large patch of black oil coming to the surface, but no further sign of the submarine. An entry in the log adds the following however: 'Cap ribbon(German) washed up on St Mary's four days later'.

There was more action on June 25 when the crew of *8665* spotted a surfaced submarine at an estimated ten miles. The U-boat submerged as the flying boat approached but three 100-lb bombs were dropped and an 'enormous bubble' was observed. Not seen again, the submarine could only be recorded as yet another 'possible'. Further sightings and attacks followed during August and October 1917 by which time it was obvious that the loudly voiced opinion that 'they would soon be back at Felixstowe' made the previous February was not to be fulfilled. The weather and sea conditions around the Scillies had certainly made things difficult but had not prevented operations, despite the amount of extra weight carried by flying boats in the form of water soaked up by their hulls during long weeks of mooring out in New Grimsby harbour. Gales were another hazard, causing chaos at Tresco on December 16 1917 when the wind reached 100 mph. A flying boat lashed to the slipway trolley threatened to lift off and the moored machines 'flew like kites' until the ropes parted, then turned turtle and drifted onto the open beach. Three H 16s were complete write-offs.

Longer range Porte F 2As were received in February 1918, followed by the much improved F 3, and it was one of the latter, *N4341*, which was on an anti-submarine patrol on May 10 when a U-boat was sighted at three miles. It rapidly submerged but two 230-lb bombs were dropped ahead of the wake and a search of the area commenced. Nothing more was seen and the *U-103* escaped. It was later sunk by the RMS *Olympic* and the commander captured. During interrogation he produced a fragment of one of the bombs dropped by *N4341*—it had lodged in the submarine casing.

Searches for missing ships were common and on occasion the large flying boats were sent out to look for lost Short 184s, though the size of the Atlantic rollers gave the latter little chance if they were forced down at sea. Short *N2963* disappeared in this way on July 6 and it was September before the body of the W/T operator was washed ashore near Ushant. The flying boats were not immune to damage either, particularly on take-off when heavily loaded machines often suffered 'bouncing'. A series of bounces resulted in the whole of the port side of the hull of F 3 *N4000* giving way on August 7 1918. The machine was beached on Samson just in time but *N4001* was not so lucky when it crashed outside the harbour on August 22.

The strength of RNAS Tresco varied considerably and it never reached the planned 12 Porte F 3s. On July 1 1918 only one F 3 and a Short 184 were available, but after the unit re-formed as No 234 Squadron in August the situation improved markedly. By the end of September, when operating as part of No 71 Wing, Penzance, under the overall control of No 9 Group, Plymouth, the unit had eight F 3s, one H 12 and two Short 184s at its disposal and nominally functioned as four separate flights, Nos 350-353.

The last of the 13 attacks made on U-boats by Tresco-based aircraft occurred on October 11, just a month before the end of the war, when the crew of H 12 *N4341* sighted a tell-tale wake four miles ahead of Convoy HH71. As usual the submarine dived before the flying boat reached the spot but bombs were dropped on the oil slick and nothing more was seen of the submarine, so the way was clear for another group of ships carrying vital supplies from America.

The penultimate wartime patrol was made on November 10—yet another convoy escort. Activity was then much reduced and finally fizzled out when No 234 Squadron disbanded in May 1919. The air station was closed but the Scillies remained on the reserve list of flying boat moorings, its usefulness being tested by the Seaplane Development Flight during August 1922. The mixed bunch of flying boats on strength included the new Short Cromarty which successfully rode out a storm moored off St Mary's, only to have the bottom of the hull torn out when it was accidentally taxied on to rocks. It was salvaged with the help of personnel from HMS *Ark Royal*, but found to be beyond economical repair.

Little further use was made of the Scillies moorings for 20 years, then it again became necessary to extend patrols further out into the Atlantic. From 1941 until 1944 detachments of Sunderlands from Nos 201, 204, 228 and 10(RAAF) Squadrons employed the trots off St Mary's and experienced similar problems to those which afflicted the 'boats' at Porth Mellon 25 years earlier. Several were damaged, and two were lost, in the sudden gales which are a feature of the Scilly Isles.

The original RNAS power house still stands on Tresco together with a number of re-roofed ex-WD huts. The concrete foundations of the long-demolished hangars are in use for new farm buildings. Stretching across the sand, the rotting remains of the slipway are still visible but have become seriously undermined by the scouring action of the sea, and will probably not last much longer. It is now a tranquil place—and it is difficult to visualize all that frantic activity 67 years ago.

Turnberry, Strathclyde (VII)

No 2 (Auxiliary) School of Air Gunnery formed here in January 1917 and disbanded on May 10 1918. No 1 School of Aerial Fighting & Gunnery formed here on May 10 1918, and was redesignated No 1 Fighting School on May 29 the same year.

Turnhouse, Lothian (VII)

Decoy Q-Site was at Ratho. Allocated to the 8th Air Force as tactical fighter base for lodger units on July 12 1943 but never occupied by the USAAF.

Upavon, Wiltshire (V)

Following the build-up of the Central Flying School during 1915 the Upavon-Andover road was virtually closed and the landing ground extended to the north. Six more 70 ft × 65 ft wooden aeroplane sheds were constructed on the eastern side of the main domestic site, and an area along the top of the escarpment forming Upavon Hill was used as a separate LG. By the end of the war the aerodrome and facilities covered a massive 3,324 acres of ground. The 14 small aeroplane sheds had been joined by three larger 140 ft × 70 ft ones along the southern side of the old Andover road and two 'plane stores' had been built to the north.

The CFS did not suffer the steady dilution experienced by other training units which were frequently required to provide nuclei for new squadrons, but in 1917 four were formed at Upavon, Nos 72 and 73 in July, No 85 in August and No 87 in September. All moved to other aerodromes almost immediately, taking with them a number of the CFS staff to fill senior squadron appointments—a loss which could be ill-afforded. By the summer of 1918, however, the CFS was operating four large training squadrons, 'A' & 'B' with Service types while 'C' & 'D' had the excellent Avro 504K for dual instruction. The unit's task was the production of single-seat fighter pilots to 'B' Standard (ie, ready for finishing school) with a monthly output of 60. It was established for six Camels, 48 Avro 504Ks and 48 SE 5As, though as usual the actual strength was much more varied.

The school remained open after the Armistice but with flying concentrated to the south of the re-opened Upavon-Andover road. Four rather undulating grass runways were marked out, the longest of 5,250 ft facing E/W. The technical accommodation was gradually improved, two of the so-called 'storage sheds' being the only First World War hangarage remaining by the mid-1930s when a secondary landing ground was opened north of the main road and called Upavon (North). Much smaller than Upavon (South), it had a maximum E/W landing run of 1,950 ft and was closed to visiting aircraft unless they were in trouble.

During the Second World War a number of Blister hangars were erected around the perimeter of the south airfield and at the end of 1944 the available hangarage consisted of two Type 'A', a single Type 'C', a Type 'L', ten Blisters and a Tunell—the latter a bit of a mystery, but in existence until July 1964, when it burnt down resulting in the loss of the unique Miles Sparrowjet which was inside at the time.

Currently the two 'A' hangars and the Type 'C' remain in good condition alongside the A342 and are used as the MT section, by No 622 Gliding School/Wyvern Gliding Club, and the Supply Flight/Hobbies Centre respectively. On the northern side of the road a mini Type 'C' Aircraft Repair Shed is in use as the gymnasium. The airfield is still in use for gliding, helicopter and fixed wing powered flying, the air traffic control being manned for notified movements.

Built in 1914, the original SHQ is now the Trenchard Museum opened during October 1983 by the present Viscount. It includes a reconstruction of the Commandant's Office and still has the wooden verandah from which the future first Chief of Air Staff, Major Hugh Trenchard, used to watch the trainees undergoing flying instruction. The museum is not open to the public but may be visited by appointment.

Some miles away from Upavon, at the junction of the A344, A360 and B3086 roads near Stonehenge (SU099429), is an ornate granite cross erected by the comrades of Captain Lorraine and Staff Sergeant Wilson. They were killed in an accident to a Nieuport monoplane at that spot while flying from Upavon on July 5 1912.

Upper Heyford, Oxfordshire (VI)

SP517268.

The F-111Es of the 20th TFW's 55th (blue), 77th (red) and 79th (yellow) Squadrons were joined late in 1983 by the 42nd Electronic Combat Squadron assigned to the 20th, and which became equipped with pale grey-camouflaged EF-111A Raven electronic warfare aircraft. On July 1 1985 the 66th Electronic Combat Wing formed at Sembach, Germany, and to this was assigned the 42nd ECS.

Upton, Dorset

SY990930. 2 miles NW of Poole on minor road off the A35.

Located just west of Upton House on the Llewellin estate, this airship sub-station was protected by trees from most directions, though the actual site was apparently fairly open. Like Toller it was opened in 1918 as a mooring-out base for SS Zero non-rigids on detachment from Mullion Airship Station. It would doubtless have been transferred to Moreton had that planned station become operational.

After the Armistice Upton was quickly abandoned.

A vertical view of Upavon camp in 1918—and much the same today (RAF Museum, P4738).

Upwood, Cambridgeshire (I)

Upwood, whose early post-war role was the accommodation of four heavy bomber squadrons equipped with 24 and later 32 aircraft, remains MoD property although it is under-utilised. Its fine pre-war buildings are partly used by US personnel from Alconbury. In wartime, for casualties in East Anglia would certainly be high, it would serve as a very necessary hospital—according to local papers.

Usworth, Tyne and Wear (VII)

No 103 Squadron moved to Abingdon on August 7 1938. The airfield closed on May 31 1984, the last movement being Rockwell Commander 112 *G-CRIL* which took off at 16.24 hours. Site clearing equipment was in action within days preparing the ground for the Nissan factory. The Beehive hangar will be retained and the North-East Aircraft Museum has moved to a site just across the road. A Pickett-Hamilton retractable fort was salvaged intact by the contractors and presented to the museum. The Japanese may succeed where the Germans failed, and the marks of bombs will survive in the fields alongside the Nissan factory; it gives many food for thought.

Valley, Anglesey (III)

The USAAF Ferry Terminal was run by the 1407th Air Base Unit and received its first aircraft, B-17F *42-30504*, direct from Newfoundland on July 25 1943. As well as the regular Transatlantic services, there was also a daily shuttle (inaugurated on October 23 1943) between Hendon, Valley, Nutts Corner, Prestwick and return with C-47s. 'White Project', the plan to redeploy the 8th Air Force from Europe to the Pacific, got under way on May 17 1945 when 12 B-24s arrived from Warton, together with 50 from the 93rd BG. By the month's end a total of 727 aircraft had been processed through Valley via the northern route through Iceland. The final total, achieved by mid-July, was 2,678. No 10 AGS re-formed here on December 1 1946 with Wellingtons and Spitfires, and disbanded on July 1 1947.

Waddington, Lincolnshire (II)

In January 1946 No 50 Squadron arrived at Waddington from Sturgate, remaining until they disbanded on January 31 1951. During their stay at Waddington No 50 Squadron detached to Binbrook from August to December 1947 and at various times to Shallufa in Egypt.

As a reminder of the station's role with the V-Force Vulcan *XM607* remains as gate guardian. Vulcan *XL426* also remained at Waddington and continued to give flying displays throughout 1985.

Top *Chipmunks, Ansons and two civilian Proctors in the 'Beehive Hangar' at Usworth in 1951* (via J. Relph).

Above *Avro 504N of 607 Squadron at Usworth in 1934* (via F. Neal).

At the end of the 1984 season it was destined for Royal Air Force Akrotiri but at the time of writing that had been postponed.

With the Vulcans gone the station now has a change of role and during August 1985 Waddington housed the Joint Training Unit with one Mark 3 AEW Nimrod. This unit incorporates the future OCU and is now embarked on a training programme. But, as the weeks pass into months and the months into years, the Nimrod grows more grotesque; by June 1985 about £831 million had been spent on the airborne early warning programme, and the aircraft was still not ready for service. Because of the continued delay in bringing the Nimrod into service, a programme of major servicing on Shackletons started at the end of 1985.

The guns and radar now equipping No 2729 (City of Lincoln) Squadron, Royal Air Force Regiment based at Waddington, were ones captured from the Argentine Army during the Falklands' campaign. The guns and their associated radar control units, and a huge quantity of ammunition captured, eventually found their way back to Britain and were dispersed to Army, Royal Navy and RAF units and museums as trophies.

The creation of the Skyguard Oerlikon Squadron of the Royal Auxiliary Air Force Regiment was the brainchild of Squadron Leader Mike Fonfe, who, while serving as the low level defence staff officer in the RAF Regiment Directorate, conceived the idea of using the captured

Swiss Oerlikon twin 35 mm anti-aircraft guns and fire control radars for the defence of an airfield in the United Kingdom. Fonfe was given the go-ahead and some £30 million worth of guns, radars and ammunition was eventually brought together to form the squadron at Waddington.

Forty years after the Second World War Royal Air Force Waddington found itself playing host to American airmen when it became the main base for the 104th, 174th and 175th Tactical Fighter Squadrons of the American National Guard, during their month-long tour of Europe as part of Operation 'Coronet Buffalo'. Flying Corsair A7s, which have co-ordination and support roles, they were in Europe to practice their function within NATO of defending northern Europe. It was the biggest-ever exercise by American part-time airmen, for two-thirds of the visiting 132 Tactical Fighter Wing were part-timers.

Below *Line-up of six Danish Drakens at RAF Waddington during 'Mallet Blow' Exercise on July 31 1985.*

Centre E-181, *an F-16A Fighting Falcon of the Danish Air Force, seen here at RAF Waddington during 'Mallet Blow' Exercise on July 31 1985.*

Bottom *Tornado GR 1s of Nos 16 and 9 Squadrons at Waddington in June 1985 during Exercise 'Enterprise'.*

Top *Two Dutch NF 5As of 314 Squadron at Waddington, both in the new Air Defence Grey colour scheme.*

Above *Single-seat Corsair A7D ground-attack specialist aircraft at Waddington.*

Below *A NATO E3A at Waddington, standing in for the 'Never-Ready' Nimrod. This aircraft could have been purchased in the first place before the Nimrod got to the 'White Elephant' stage. Note that 'OTAN' is 'NATO' backwards.*

Waltham, Lincolnshire (II)

The wartime airfield at Waltham remains much the same but interest in the old airfield has grown over the years. In September 1981 the Royal Air Force Waltham Association was formed, not by a veteran of those far-off wartime days, but by a young man, 21 years of age, by the name of Ian Reid. He decided to form the Association in order to meet the men and women who made Waltham their home during the war years. The first reunion was held in 1982 and was a huge success. In July 1985 a group of Canadians who served with 100 Squadron at Waltham had a mini-reunion and planned to return in 1987. For the 1985 reunion 100 Squadron (flying Canberras) attended, thus forming the link of past and present members of the first night-bombing squadron formed.

Warton, Lancashire (III)

The 2025th Gunnery Flight was present here from July 6 1943 to December 14 1943 with Lysanders and Masters. It was redesignated as the 1st Gunnery & Tow Target Flight on August 26 1943 and moved to Templeton on December 14 1943.

Watchet, Somerset

ST092432. 1 mile E of Watchet off A39 road.

During the 1920s the Army established an anti-aircraft gunnery range off the coast near Watchet and used it during the summer months for large-scale training camps. The targets were towed by aircraft operating from Weston Zoyland, a landing ground some 19 miles to the east, but communications between the two camps were so poor that a piece of flattish land was cleared alongside the AA training area for use by light liaison aircraft. Horsleys were initially used as drogue towers and soon after the Night Flying Flight took over this work in 1929 one of their aircraft crashed on the strip. More usual visitors were Avro 504s, Tomtits and DH 60 Moths, however, one of the latter coming to grief when it hit telephone wires soon after taking off from Watchet on July 2 1931.

Firing at drogues towed on a constant heading at a steady speed and height had limited value. Aiming live rounds at a manoeuvring target was what was required and when the pilotless, radio-controlled DH Queen Bee (a modified Tiger Moth) became available in July 1935 the Anti-Aircraft Co-operation Flight started flight trials. There were many frustrating problems to overcome but an operational detachment from No 1 AACU was sent down to Watchet in July 1937 and the first pilotless launch was made on August 3 from a catapult set up at Doniford, close to the Army camp. This was successful, but the machine was damaged on landing on the waters of the Bristol Channel and a month later it was written off following a catapult accident. The unit returned in greater strength in May 1938 when 'Z' Flight arrived by train and flew no less than eight Queen Bees. One was lost on July 20 when it crashed into the sea, and another was shot down during August. The survivors returned to Henlow in October for winter storage.

Re-formed in May 1939, 'Z' Flight moved immediately to Watchet and was joined from Weybourne by 'X' Flight in September. The outbreak of war resulted in training continuing through the winter but a year later both Flights left for ranges in Wales. Only one Queen Bee suffered an accident during the detachment, but four were destroyed by the gunners—either they were getting better shots or it was a matter of quantity rather than quality! All firing now concentrated on drogues towed by Hawker Henleys. These operated out of Weston Zoyland, but the Watchet strip remained open and Lysanders of No 16 Squadron often flew in using their renowned 'skyhook' short landing techniques. When the American Army started using the facilities their Piper L-4 Cubs were also frequent visitors.

After the war there was considerable indecision over the fate of Watchet but it became the Light Anti-Aircraft Gunnery School of the RAF Regiment in July 1947, No 15 (LAA) Squadon moving in from Nethertown. They were transferred to Upavon in December but were replaced by No 16 (LAA) Squadron which formed at Watchet on January 12 1948. During the early 1950s they were joined by LAA Auxiliary squadrons of the RAF Regiment, these units spending part of their annual 14-day summer camps at Watchet.

The defence cuts of 1956 resulted in the disbandment of the Auxiliaries and a trim back in regular RAF Regiment strength. With Army ranges then able to accommodate the gunners' requirements, Watchet was closed in February 1957.

Waterbeach, Cambridgeshire (I)

Mr G.D. Collings of Hull wrote pointing out some errors in Volume 1 relating to the loss of 'Q' Queenie of 99 Squadron. The aircraft took off at 02.00 on December 8 1941 and at 600 ft, just after take-off, an explosion occurred in the starboard engine. Apparently a cylinder head had blown off, and fuel still being pumped into the cylinder caused a fierce fire. Without two engines functioning height could not be maintained. As soon as the other aircraft were away 'Q' Queenie, of which Mr Collings was co-pilot, turned on to finals and then the starboard engine failed producing a long trail of fire. The Wellington simply ran out of airspace and crashed on to a newly ploughed field just short of the runway. Five of the six crew members survived, and 'Q' Queenie exploded about a minute after the crash.

Waterbeach remains an active Army centre amid constant rumours that part of the one-time landing ground is to be sold for agricultural use.

Wattisham, Suffolk (I)

TM022516.

Wattisham was one of the first post-war expansion airfields to have ASPs and ORPs. July 1950 saw its long runway opened making way for Meteors of 257 and 263 Squadrons before an all-weather squadron completed the Wattisham Wing. Its standby station was Stradishall.

Wattisham remains an RAF Phantom station although it was denied one of its squadrons when, on March 30 1983, the 29 Squadron detachment at Port Stanley in the Falklands was renumbered 23 Squadron. Wattisham's '23' promptly surrendered its Phantoms to Coningsby, perhaps because 29 Squadron had already been chosen as the first to fly Tornado fighters. Only 56 Squadron's Phantoms remained at Wattisham until on July 31 1984 74 Squadron re-formed. These, re-vamped US Navy F-4Js, the first of which arrived on August 30 1984, have General Electric J-79 engines with modifications to reduce smoke emission and a missile control system as fitted to the US Navy's F-14 Tomcats. The F-4J(UK) Phantoms wear a slightly bluer grey finish than 56 Squadron's F-4M Rolls-Royce Spey-powered Phantom FGR 2s, and carry either four Sidewinder or four Sparrow missiles.

Wellesbourne Mountford, Warwickshire (VI)

Wellesbourne attracts a variety of flying for fun, but has not as yet reached its potential for such activity. The west ends of asphalt runway 05/23, 1,627 ft long and 59 ft wide, and 36/18 of 2,992 ft long and 75 ft wide are available for flying.

Weston-super-Mare, Somerset (V)

When No 286 Squadron left Weston-super-Mare in December 1943 it was replaced by a detachment of Oxfords from No 116 Squadron, Croydon. This detachment was built up to 12 aircraft, employed mainly on the calibration of anti-aircraft gun radars all over south-west England and southern Wales. It was steady if rather monotonous work, lightened by brief sightings of the massed supply convoys setting course for France after D-Day, and darkened by the occasional accident. One very unpleasant crash occurred when an Oxford failed to pull out of a steep dive over the airfield and hit the ground near the gasworks. The pilot and groundcrew passenger were both killed.

Squadron personnel were billeted in huts on the airfield boundary near the old Western Airways hangar and the main entrance.

Westward Ho, Devon

SS443307. 2½ miles N of Bideford off minor road.

A romantic sounding name and an extraordinary shape were about the only noteworthy attributes of this landing ground, established early in 1918 to operate ex-trainer DH 6s on coastal patrol work.

The chosen site was a golf course on Northam Burrows, a low-lying promontory sticking out into the entrance to the River Taw. Covering some 90 acres, it was in the shape of a frying pan, a 1,050-ft radius circle with a 'handle' extension lying in a south-westerly direction towards Goosey Pool and the village of Westward Ho. All the accommodation was temporary, the machines being housed in Bessoneaux hangars and the personnel in Armstrong huts. A large wooden shed served as guardroom and mess.

The 12 DH 6 biplanes were divided between two Flights, Nos 502 and 503 (Special Duty). They were operational by June 1918 and in August were absorbed by the newly formed No 260 Squadron,

RAF, though still retaining their separate identities. They spent the rest of the war plodding up and down the north Devon coast at 20-minute intervals, seeing no enemy activity but hopefully keeping any U-boat in the vicinity submerged and thus unable to operate efficiently.

The squadron disbanded on February 22 1919 and with the temporary buildings removed the golf links were rapidly restored to their former glory. Signs of military habitation of the site are few, but no doubt the daily sight and sound of Hawks from nearby Chivenor stirs the memories of some of the older inhabitants.

Westwood (Peterborough), Cambridgeshire

See Peterborough.

Wheaton Aston, Staffordshire (III)

The 'T1' hangars have been removed. The Battle HQ exists on a small knoll near the north-east perimeter track close to the machine-gun butts and an unusual (for a training station) dispersal pen. Most of the dispersed living sites have been cleared apart from the Communal Site with its cookhouse.

Whitchurch Heath (Tilstock), Shropshire

See Tilstock.

Wick, Highland (VII)

No 618 Squadron reached Wick on July 9 1944. An unusual feature of Wick is that the tower and most technical buildings are made largely of timber. The document issued in 1984 by the Civil Aviation Authority describing the Scottish airfields up for disposal notes that one hangar and about 13 acres of land and other buildings at Wick are surplus to present aviation requirements.

Windermere (Bowness), Cumbria (III)

Also known as Bowness. The modified Falcon II which made the first glider take-off from water on February 3 1942 can be seen at the Windermere Steamboat Museum. The hangar bases and adjoining roads and hardstandings are now a caravan site. The Short Shetland prototype, *DX166*, alighted on the lake on January 13 1945.

Wittering, Cambridgeshire (VI)

TF032027.

Reader David Benfield reminded us that in 1912 the famous B.C. Hucks gave a flying display in Burghley Park, close to Wittering. Also, a Mr Glue purchased the well-known Blackburn Monoplane and flew it from Wittering Heath between 1912 and 1914. Mr Benfield also pointed out that the long runway linking Colly Weston and Wittering opened in 1941. 'Colly' was built on a site known in the 1914-18 war as Easton on the Hill and was still known by that name when it re-opened for tests of Q-Site and K-Site decoys in September 1939.

Woodbridge, Suffolk (I)

TM333492.

Woodbridge retains its huge wartime asphalt 09/27 runway of which 9,000 ft remains in use allowing almost 1,000 ft for overshoots. It is an active USAF base, home of the A-10As of the 78th and 91st Squadrons of the 81st Tactical Fighter Wing. Additionally, it has a more individualistic role as the base of the 67th Air Recovery & Rescue Squadron nominally equipped with four Sikorsky HH-53C 'Jolly Green Giant' helicopters and four specially modified Lockheed HC-130N/P Hercules.

Woodford, Cheshire (III)

No 184 Gliding School was present here for various periods in 1944/45.

Woolsington, Northumberland (VII)

No 27 Gliding School had formed here by October 1943, and moved to Ouston in June 1948. Towards the end of May 1946 No 63 MU, a salvage unit, moved here from a ground station at Carluke in Scotland.

Worcester, Hereford and Worcester (III)

When 2 EFTS moved into Staverton in August 1940, they did most of their flying from Worcester from then onwards. HQ and Administration staff eventually moved to Worcester in June 1942. No 81 Group Communication Flight was present from February to December 1941. No 2 EFTS left for Yatesbury in August 1945.

Wrexham, Clwyd (III)

First used from July to late 1940 as a RLG for 5 SFTS, Sealand.

Wroughton, Wiltshire (IX)

Another unit for the expanding Royal Auxiliary Air Force was formed on September 9 1983—an Aeromedical Evacuation Squadron consisting of 13 medical officers, 23 nursing sisters and 168 airmen/airwomen attached to the Princess Mary's Hospital, Wroughton. As the name implies it is intended as a back-up for the full-time casualty care and air evacuation organisation.

The Science Museum airliner collection at Wroughton has also increased in size, and now boasts 16 different types of aircraft. It has been relocated in two hangars on the north side of the airfield, the move in March 1984 giving enthusiasts a rare opportunity to see the aircraft in the open air. Though now back under cover, the airliners are well displayed and regular open days provide the chance to view some famous machines at close quarters.

Wye, Kent (IX)

The excellent book *The Air Defence of Britain 1914-18* (Putnam) reveals many fascinating facets of the contemporary World War 1 scene, not least the involvement of Wye in home defence. Several new squadrons were formed during the early months of 1916 following the transfer of responsibilty for air defence from the Admiralty to the War Office. Amongst them was No 50 Squadron, RFC, based at Dover but intended to operate dispersed Flights, one of them at Wye.

In fact the plan was changed and it was almost a year later that the aerodrome found itself host to a home defence unit, albeit a part-time one! This was No 65 Squadron, a scout unit working up on DH 5s at Wye in preparation for operations on the Western Front. Following the first daylight raid on Britain by the Gothas of Kagohl 3 it was required, like similar squadrons elsewhere, to make pilots and aircraft available to the Home Defence Group on demand.

Two DH 5s were among the varied types which took off in a vain attempt to intercept 22 Gothas attacking Sheerness on June 5 1917. There was a repeat performance eight days later, and yet again on July 4, by which time Camels were re-equipping the squadron. Altogether eight sorties were mounted during the Gotha daylight offensive of 1917 before the dedicated home defence unit strength was considered sufficient to allow the 'amateurs' to get on with their proper task—and Wye to concentrate on training.

Wyton, Cambridgeshire (I)

TL288749.

Wyton will surely pass into history as 'The Home of the Canberra'. Apart from a few examples used for experimental work the remaining British Canberras are Wyton-based. Prominent still are the bull-nosed T 17 electronic warfare trainers of 360 Squadron which arrived from Cottesmore

A BE 2B of a Training Squadron in the pleasant surroundings of Wye aerodrome (Captain D.S. Glover via P.H.T. Green).

An unhappy-looking BE 2C after yet another training accident at Wye. Note the metal-framed, corrugated-iron clad aeroplane sheds typical of the period prior to the general introduction of the GS hangar (Captain D.S. Glover via P.H.T. Green).

in August 1975 and now boldly wear squadron colours, and the mixture of B 2s, T 4s, PR 7s and TT Mk 18 yellow and black-striped target towers which equip 100 Squadron which arrived in January 1982 after absorbing 7 Squadron to provide more target facilities. A further handful of B 2s and T 4s arm 231 Operational Training Unit. Additional to these on this No 18 (Maritime) Group station are the PR 9s of the small No 1 PRU. It re-formed in October 1982 from the remains of No 13 which, with a dozen Canberra PR 7s, moved in from Malta on October 3 1978 and assumed a low-level tactical reconnaissance/night photography role. Its disbandment here on January 5 1982 was followed by that of 39 Squadron on May 28 1982. No 1 PRU re-formed in October 1982, from the remains of these two squadrons, for photographic duties both civilian and military.

June 1984 saw the Service withdrawal of the Devon and 207 Squadron's Wyton detachment died. It had arrived in February 1969 as 26 Squadron which, upon disbandment in February 1976, became a detached Flight of 207 Squadron. Also on the station is the Electronic Warfare and Avionics Unit which came from Watton in 1970 and undertakes trials and special installation work. Since April 1983 Wyton has become directly defended by Bloodhound 2s of B Flight, 25 Squadron, which has it headquarters here and maintains its C Flight at Wattisham. Bloodhounds, can, incidentally, also be seen on the skyline at West Raynham and these belong to 85 Squadron.

No indisputable evidence has come to light to confirm that Wyton's Q-Site at Somersham, about two miles south of Pidley and two miles north-east of Woodhurst, was ever used for practice landings by Tempsford's inmates despite persistent tales.

Wyton has seen numerous changes in recent years. The last Victor SR 2 of 543 Squadron left the station on April 3 1975. The following year 51 Squadron's last Canberra, *WT305*, a modified Mk 6, was placed by Wyton's Main Gate where it doubtless keeps an eye on people entering—and upon its PR 7 colleague, *WH773*.

Much of Wyton's activity is heavily classified, none more so than the activities of the Nimrod R 1s of 51 Squadron, the first of which moved in during 1971 and flew its first operational sortie on May 3 1974. Their Baltic prowls have been photographed by the Swedes and doubtless less friendly souls, but their existence is about all that British officialdom admits to... except when on Wyton's open days it parks a Nimrod tantalisingly distantly or displays a huge but aged photograph of one in a hangar show!

Yate, Gloucestershire (V)

The Luftwaffe's interest in Parnalls' Yate factory did not end with the attempted raid of September 27 1940. As vividly portrayed in the booklet *Gloucestershire at War 1939-45* by Derek Archer (F. Bailey & Son Ltd, 1979) a few stray bombs which dropped nearby on December 7 blew in many windows, but much more serious was the low level attack by a single He 111 on February 27 1941. In broad daylight, using the distinctive railway network to pinpoint the factory, the crew laid six HE bombs across the factory, causing considerable damage to the drawing office and turret shop, killing 52 and injuring many more of the 4,000-plus workers at Parnall's

This audacious attack led to plans for some sections to be dispersed to other premises in the area, but before action could be taken a second raid on March 7 caused much more damage and killed three more workers—a timely siren alert giving most personnel time to reach the shelters. The MAP ordered immediate complete dispersal and Boulton Mills, Dursley, was taken over as one of the main production centres. Heavy machinery and tons of equipment were removed from Yate in a fleet of lorries and eight days after the second bombing attack Parnall's factory was an empty shell and the dispersed sites were starting up production. The flow of gun turrets to bomber factories was hardly interrupted.

Eye witnesses confirm that Parnall's Hendy Hecks continued to use the airfield for liaison work throughout the war. Some of the remaining facilities were used by the Army regimental training courses.

Yatesbury, Wiltshire (V)

During World War 1 Yatesbury consisted of two almost equally sized landing grounds alongside the present A4 and divided by the minor road leading to the village. The western aerodrome covered 260 acres and had a large technical site on its northern boundary, three of the 1915-pattern 'Single Span' hangars still being in existence. The eastern field had its maintenance facilities concentrated in the south-west corner close to the intersection of the village access road and the A4—and has disappeared completely.

No 55 Reserve Squadron arrived from Filton in November 1916 as the first unit to be based at Yatesbury. Early in 1917 it was joined by other RSs and by late 1918 Yatesbury was the HQ of No 28 Wing, No 7 Group, RAF, and was occupied by Nos 36 and 37 TDS. Both operated two training squadrons instructing corps reconnaissance courses, the total establishment of the unit being 48 Avro 504Ks and 48 RE 8s.

Following the re-opening of Yatesbury in 1936 a large side-opening hangar of the 'Northern Lights' type was built on the eastern edge of the western airfield and new domestic accommodation was erected for the Bristol School. When the Radio School was approved during the summer of 1939 a huge hutted camp was built on what had been the eastern landing ground of World War 1—the strength of the unit reaching thousands. During 1941-42 three 2,700 ft Sommerfeld Track runways were laid on the 'western' airfield together with a perimeter track which gave access to dispersed Blister hangars. These numbered 11 by 1944 and provided some much needed extra cover for the numerous Proctors on strength. A single Bellman was also erected near the 'Northern Lights' hangar.

The remaining hangars at Yatesbury, while not unique, are unusual in being well-preserved and are worthy of a visit. Permission to view them closely must be requested, however, firstly from the manager of the road haulage contractors depot using the 'Northern Lights' hangar and secondly from the occupier of the first house on the access road to the World War 1 sheds and remains of the northern domestic site.

Yeadon (Leeds/Bradford), Yorkshire (IV)

For many months the contractors have been hard at work at Leeds-Bradford Airport, laying new roads and erecting new buildings. In 1984 the airport's 1,800-yd main runway (15/33) was extended to 2,460 yd to take full intercontinental flights. The width has been retained at 50 yd. A British Airways Boeing 747 was the first Jumbo to land on Leeds-Bradford's newly lengthened runway. An Airtours TriStar was the fourth to land there and the airport is able to cope with all the big jets except Concorde. The extended runway now means that some of the types of aircraft currently using the airport can do so more economically by operating at maximum payload. The money spent—some £23 million —on the extension programme has been worth while for carriers had estimated that by not being able to operate at maximum payload they had a penalty of up to £30 per seat added to their operating costs. The new extension removed that penalty, and it is predicted that by 1990 more than 800,000 people will be passing through the airport each year.

Top *The 1915-pattern 'Single Span' hangars under construction at Yatesbury in April 1917, close to the large hutted camp on the northern side of the aerodrome* (E.F. Cheesman).

Above *One of the self-same 'Single Span' hangars at Yatesbury, today still in pristine condition.*

Below *A FE 2B 'pusher' bomber at Yatesbury—backed by a Bessoneau and the 'Single Span' hangars* (RAF Museum, P8608).

Yeovilton, Somerset (V)

The birth pangs of most Second World War airfields were painful, but few suffered as much as Yeovilton, conceived in 1938 and born prematurely in the dark days of 1940 following the rapidly changing situation on the Continent which produced equally dramatic changes of plan at home. The first hangars on the site were erected early in 1940 and on completion were handed over to Westland Aircraft Ltd as a sub-site of their Yeovil factory. Work on the airfield was pressed forward as rapidly as possible but before the runways could be completed a party of 'maintainers' from the Observer School at Ford moved in and from May 1940 onwards the unit's aircraft were flown over daily for dispersal. With difficulty they were able to continue training, operating from the grass areas of the airfield, but the Observer School itself remained at Ford until the autumn of 1940 when it moved north to Arbroath.

There was one Luftwaffe attack—by a stray Ju 88 which bombed the Westland facility, causing some damage and injuries, but it was September 1940 before the Fleet Fighter School (759 and 760 Squadrons) assembled at Yeovilton and the airfield was put in some semblance of order. The Westland (Ilchester) works had already become a major repair centre for damaged Spitfires and now started modifying ex-French contract Mohawks and Tomahawks. Later the conversion of Lysanders for clandestine 'Special Operations'—the landing of agents in enemy-occupied territory—was undertaken, but the main activity for the rest of the war concerned repair and assembly of Spitfires and Seafires.

Meanwhile 787 Squadron was formed at Yeovilton with ex-804 Squadron aircrew, three Fulmars and five Gladiators on March 5 1941 as the Fleet Fighter Development Unit. It did not stay long, moving to Duxford on June 18.

When the Henstridge satellite opened in April 1943 the opportunity was taken to rationalise Naval fighter training, 759 Squadron remaining at Yeovilton as No 1 Naval Fighter School while No 2 NAFS was formed on the new station. No 1 NAFS concentrated on Hurricanes and Martlets at first, changing later to the 'crank-wing' Corsair of which some 150 were on strength in 1945! With the ending of Lend-Lease the mighty Corsairs rapidly disappeared and were replaced by the dainty Seafire, these remaining until the unit disbanded.

The Maintenance Test Pilots School reached Yeovilton from Middle Wallop in April 1946 and flew Fireflies, Barracudas, Harvards, Sea Otters and even an Oxford, as well as Seafires. The object was to give training on a wide variety of types so that unit test pilots were prepared for anything which might appear on the flight line. This work continued until September 30 1949 when the unit disbanded.

In recent years Yeovilton has successfully coped with the traumas produced by the Falklands' conflict and the steadily increasing Sea Harrier and Commando Sea King commitments. The FRADU has also been updated by the arrival of Falcon 20DC twin jets. These aircraft are replacing the Canberras previously operated, but will continue to be owned by Flight Refuelling Ltd, the company which took over the FRADU contract from Airwork Ltd in December 1983.

No 3 Commando Brigade Air Squadron moved in from Coypool, Plymouth, in 1982 and operates Lynx and Gazelle helicopters. They work closely with the Fleet Air Arm whose 845 and 846 Squadrons provide the Royal Marine Brigade with assault Wessex and Sea King 'heavy lift' support. Yeovilton is the largest Naval air station in the United Kingdom, the home base for nine squadrons and nearly 120 aircraft. Over 3,000 Service and civilian personnel are employed at the base.

Zeals, Wiltshire (V)

Zeals was allocated to the 8th Air Force, USAAF, as a fighter base in August 1942 but this was cancelled the following month. In 1943 it was re-allotted to the Americans and became Station 450, the first 9th AF personnel arriving on August 1 to prepare for the establishment of a Tactical Air Depot. No 1 TAD and its support services moved in at the end of October, joined early in November by the 21st Weather Squadron, a unit which provided meteorological observer detachments on airfields of the 9th AF.

The bad autumn weather turned the airfield into a mud bath and understandably the Americans disliked Zeals intensely. No 1 TAD left on January 9 1944 but was immediately replaced by No 5 TAD whose 56 officers and 1,000 men suffered for two months until moving to Chilbolton on

Yeovilton on 'Air Day' in the 1980s, the static aircraft display dominated by the mighty C-5A Galaxy. The varied hangarage on this major FAA base is very much in evidence (HMS *Heron*).

March 11 1944. The RAF then used Zeals for just a year before the Fleet Air Arm took it over on April 14 1945 for Corsair training as part of No 1 Naval Air Fighter School, Yeovilton. The Corsair was an awe-inspiring brute and the crowded circuit at Yeovilton had proved no place for initial practice, so 760 Squadron formed a familiarisation Flight at Zeals. New pilots were taught the Corsair approach, 'left wing down and a bit of top rudder', using Harvards before being let loose on the 'bent-wing bastard' in the comparative peace of this large grass airfield.

The students were housed in requisitioned cottages in the area. These were not de luxe establishments, it being said that they were rat-infested—and pilots slept with their boots on!

Zeals was unusual in having the eight oversize Blisters and single 'T1' hangar grouped together off the southern perimeter track. The public toilets in a A303 layby to the east of Zeals village are on the site of the Teeside—at least these foundations are being put to some good use!

Index

It became apparent during the indexing of the *Action Stations* series that much information did not require indexing. What most readers wished to be able to do was follow squadron movements from one volume of the series to another, in order to piece together a complete picture of their careers in a way not available through other books. This index is therefore a complete reference to each squadron as it appears in all ten volumes coupled with an index to all the airfields mentioned, facilitating that task. RAF and USAAF/USAF Groups and Wings are included on the same basis, as are Luftwaffe units, but minor units (with the exception of those mentioned in this tenth volume) are excluded since they are fully indexed in the earlier nine individual books. There is also an index of personalities.

In the following listings Roman numerals indicate volume number, and bold numerals indicate main entry.

Airfields

Personalities

The following index of personalities featured in *Action Stations 1-10* is of necessity incomplete. Is — for example — F/O Smith (with no initials) in Vol 1 in 1940 the same person as Flt Lt Smith in Vol 7 in 1943? For this reason, this part of the index is restricted to positively identifiable people, especially those highly decorated (eg. VC or GC winners) whose exploits are described; and 'celebrities' (eg Glenn Miller). No offence is intended towards those brave men (and women) mentioned in the ten *Action Stations* Volumes whose names have been omitted, and sole responsibility for errors and/or omissions lies with the editor. Where a name occurs without a rank, but with the letters (vr), it indicates that the person's rank varies according to the time of entry — for example, from P/O to Wg Cdr.

RAF Groups

RAF, RFC and RN Wings

Royal Air Force Squadrons

The numbering of RAF Squadrons is a complex subject. The following list embraces all regular RAF squadrons (numbered 1 to 200, many of which were originally RFC, and 201-299, many of which were similarly ex-RNAS); plus those in the 300 series which were largely allocated to 'Free' squadrons (ie, French or Dutch, etc); and in the 400 series (which went to Empire squadrons — Nos 400-443 being Canadian, 450-467 Australian and 480-490 New Zealand). Squadron numbers in the 500 series were originally intended for special reserve squadrons, and those in the 600s for RAuxAF squadrons, but many were allocated to regular wartime units, in the latter case particularly to Army co-operation squadrons. Not all squadron numbers were allocated and some served exclusively overseas, hence their omission.

Fleet Air Arm Squadrons

USAAF/USAF Groups

USAF Wings

USAF/USAAF Squadrons

Luftwaffe units

Miscellaneous units (*Actions Stations 10* only)

Action Stations

This popular series of books is unique in aeronautical literature. It recognises the existence of a vast army of enthusiasts who, though not necessarily interested in the aircraft themselves, DO have a very real craving for the history, and stories of heroism, that belong to their own local airfields — the **'Action Stations'.**

Action Stations 1
Military Airfields of East Anglia
Fascinating details of all 111 airfields.

Action Stations 2
Lincolnshire and the East Midlands
The 105 airfields which bore the brunt of the offensive against the 3rd Reich.

Action Stations 3
Wales and the North-West
Includes the 4 sea-plane bases.

Action Stations 4
Yorkshire
The moors, mud and mist of all 91 airfields.

Action Stations 5
The South-West
Includes Guernsey and Jersey which were under enemy occupation.

Action Stations 6
The Cotswolds and the Central Midlands
Includes Cardington, Edgehill and Old Warden.

Action Stations 7
Scotland, the North East and Northern Ireland
Covers the winning of the U-boat war.

Action Stations 8
Greater London
Deals in depth with the Battle of Britain.

Action Stations 9
Central South and South-East
Includes airfields used in the Normandy invasion.